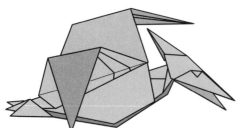

# Dinosaur Origami

## John Montroll

Dover Publications, Inc.
New York

*To Carol Ann, Kathleen, Martha, Mark, Jan, and Mark*

*Bibliographical Note*

This work is first published in 2010 in separate editions by Antroll Publishing Company, Maryland, and Dover Publications, Inc., Mineola, New York.

*Library of Congress Cataloging-in-Publication Data*

Montroll, John.
    Dinosaur origami / John Montroll.
        p. cm.
    ISBN-13: 978-0-486-47780-0
    ISBN-10: 0-486-47780-0
    1. Origami. 2. Dinosaurs in art. I. Title.
TT870.M555327 2010
736'.982—dc22

2010012096

Manufactured in the United States of America
Dover Publications, Inc., 31 East 2nd Street, Mineola, N.Y. 11501

# Introduction

inosaurs are very interesting creatures. It is fun to create them through origami. This collection is a revision of the former book *Prehistoric Origami*. Ten models from that book remain here along with twenty new ones. The models, each folded from a single uncut square, were designed to reflect an accurate and aesthetically pleasing rendition of these prehistoric animals.

You can fold the flying reptiles such as pteranodon, marine reptiles, and an assortment of favorite dinosaurs including tyrannosaurus, apatosaurus, triceratops, stegosaurus, and more. The models are roughly ordered from simple to difficult. There is also information about each animal.

The diagrams conform to the internationally approved Randlett-Yoshizawa style. Although any square paper can be used for the projects in this book, the best material is origami paper. Origami supplies can be found in arts and craft shops, or visit Dover Publications online at www.doverpublications.com, or OrigamiUSA at www.origami-usa.org.

Martha Landy has provided an excellent introduction and background notes on the animals. Ms. Landy teaches students with special needs and has produced "Dinosaur Day" for many years. Her students research and explain dinosaurs and celebrate them. She continues to love discovering new things about these Mesozoic friends and believes that they are one of the most motivating educational tools.

I thank Martha Landy for bringing this work to life with her articles. I thank Robert Lang for use of his software, ReferenceFinder, used in folding the triceratops.

I hope you will enjoy folding and making scenes of these ancient creatures.

John Montroll

www.johnmontroll.com

# Contents

**Mountain & Volcano**
★
*page 12*

**Cracked Dinosaur Egg**
★
*page 14*

**Prehistoric Tree**
★
*page 16*

**Pterodactylus**
★★
*page 18*

**Quetzalcoatlus**
★★
*page 21*

**Pteranodon**
★★★
*page 23*

**Rhamphorynchus**
★★★
*page 27*

**Elasmosaurus**
★★
*page 33*

**Tanystropheus**
★★
*page 36*

**Riojasaurus**
★★
*page 39*

**Apatosaurus**
★★
*page 42*

**Brachiosaurus**
★★
*page 45*

**Diplodocus**
★★
*page 48*

**Dimetrodon**
★★★
*page 51*

**Spinosaurus**
★★
*page 56*

# To Define a Dinosaur

To call an animal a dinosaur there are three specific criteria that must be met. These are when the animal lived, the structure of the hip and jaw bones, and where the animal spent its time.

Dinosaurs lived in the Mesozoic (mezz-oh-ZO-ik) Era which began 225 millions years ago and lasted for 155 million years. Mesozoic means "middle life". The era is divided into three periods.

Dinosaurs appeared on Earth during the Triassic (try-AS-ik) Period. It lasted for 45 million years. All the continents were connected in one giant land mass. There were only a few kinds of dinosaur. These were mostly small, quick, meat eaters.

The Jurassic (joo-RAS-ik) Period began 180 million years ago and lasted for 45 million years. The continents began to move apart and shallow seas and swamps formed. The climate was tropical. The largest dinosaurs lived at this time.

The Cretaceous (kre-TAY-shus) Period is the time the most varieties of dinosaurs lived. It was 65 million years long. The continents were well separated. The climate was seasonal and flowers appeared on earth for the first time.

To be a dinosaur an animal must have a specific skull and hip structure. One way scientists classify reptiles is by the number of holes in the back of the skull. These holes may be to accommodate jaw muscles. They lighten the weight of the skull. All dinosaurs are diapsids (di-AP-sids), having two holes in their skulls.

The Ornithischian (orn-i-THIS-kee-an) dinosaurs have the two lower bones of the hip pointing towards the back. They have a beak-like addition to the jaw bone. Ornithischian means "bird hipped".

The Saurischian (saw-RIS-kee-an) dinosaurs have each hip bone pointing in a different direction. They have a solid jaw. Saurischian means "lizard-hipped".

All true dinosaurs were land dwellers. However, some dinosaurs, like many other land dwelling animals, would sometimes wade or swim. Hollow-boned, feathered dinosaurs may have used their aerodynamic structure to glide from trees or cliffs but did not "flap" their wings and could not fly.

Recent discoveries have shown that although some dinosaurs laid eggs, some actually gave birth to live offspring. There is also evidence that some dinosaurs raised their young and lived in multi-aged family groups.

It has been over 60 million years since the last living dinosaur walked the earth but paleontologists are continuing to uncover clues that increase our understanding of the world of dinosaurs.

Martha Landy

*The Tyrannosaurus is an Ornithischian dinosaur which lived during the Cretaceous Period.*

*The Apatosaurus is a Saurischian dinosaur which lived during the Jurassic Period.*

# Symbols

## Lines

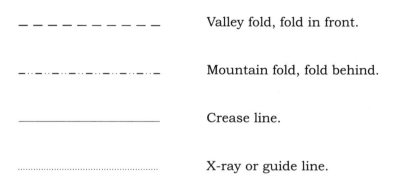

— — — — — — — — — —  Valley fold, fold in front.

— ·· — · — · — ·· — ·· —  Mountain fold, fold behind.

————————————  Crease line.

..........................................  X-ray or guide line.

## Arrows

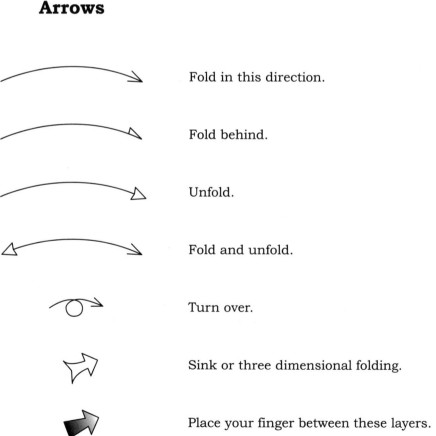

Fold in this direction.

Fold behind.

Unfold.

Fold and unfold.

Turn over.

Sink or three dimensional folding.

Place your finger between these layers.

# Basic Folds

**Rabbit Ear.**

To fold a rabbit ear, one corner is folded in half and laid down to a side.

1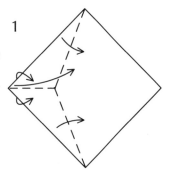

2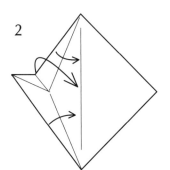

3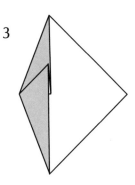

Fold a rabbit ear.          A 3D intermediate step.

**Double Rabbit Ear.**

If you were to bend a straw you would be folding the double rabbit ear.

1 2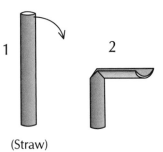

(Straw)

1 2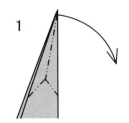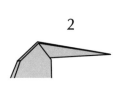

Make a double rabbit ear.

**Squash Fold.**

In a squash fold, some paper is opened and then made flat. The shaded arrow shows where to place your finger.

1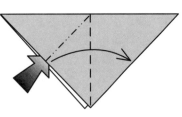

2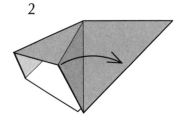

3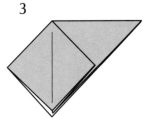

Squash-fold.          A 3D intermediate step.

**Petal Fold.**

In a petal fold, one point is folded up while two opposite sides meet each other.

1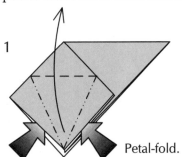

2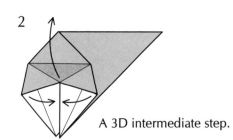

3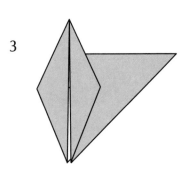

Petal-fold.          A 3D intermediate step.

## Inside Reverse Fold.

In an inside reverse fold, some paper is folded between layers. Here are two examples.

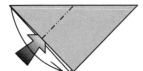

Reverse-fold.

Reverse-fold.

## Outside Reverse Fold.

Much of the paper must be unfolded to make an outside reverse fold.

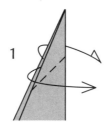

Outside-reverse-fold.

## Crimp Fold.

A crimp fold is a combination of two reverse folds.

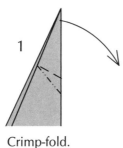

Crimp-fold.

## Sink Fold.

In a sink fold, some of the paper without edges is folded inside. To do this fold, much of the model must be unfolded.

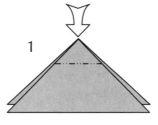

Sink.

## Spread Squash Fold.

A cross between a squash fold and sink fold, some paper in the center is spread apart and then made flat.

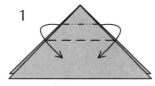

Spread-squash-fold.

# Mountain and Volcano

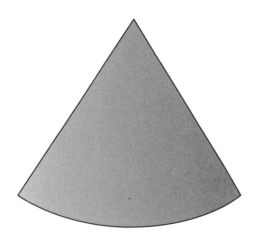

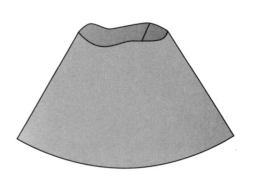

**1**

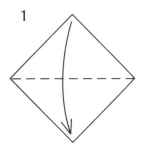

**2**

**3**

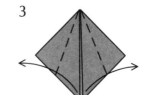

**4**

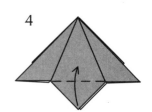

Fold both layers
up together.

**5**

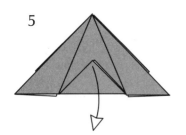

Unfold both layers.

**6**

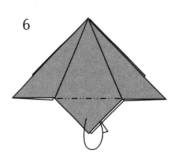

Fold the top layer inside.

**7**

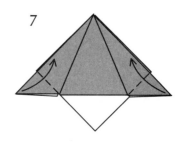

**8**

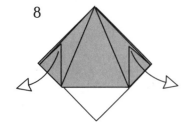

Unfold.

**9**

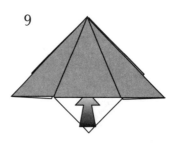

In step 11, some paper will
be tucked inside this pocket.

**10**

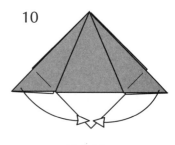

Unfold.

**11**

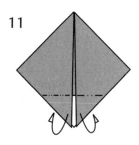

Tuck inside the pocket.

**12**

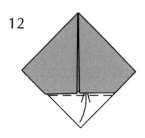

Tuck inside the pocket.

**13**

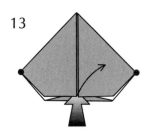

Place your finger inside to open and flatten the model so the dots meet.

**14**

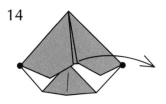

An intermediate step.

**15**

Fold the corners inside, repeat behind.

**16**

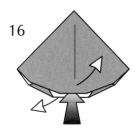

Open.

**17**

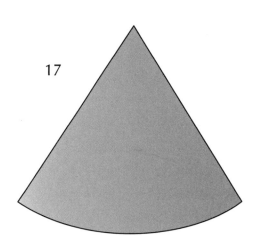

Mountain

**18**

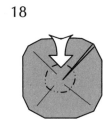

This is the top view of the mountain. To fold a volcano, push the top inside. This is a sink fold.

**19**

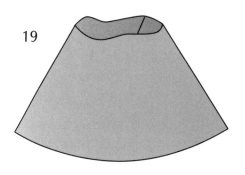

Volcano

# Cracked Dinosaur Egg

1
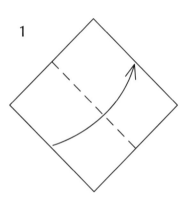

2
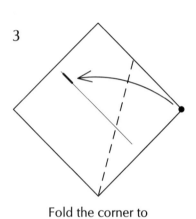

Unfold.

3
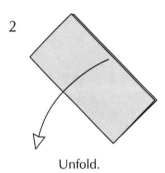

Fold the corner to the center line.

4
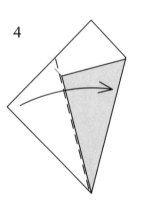

5
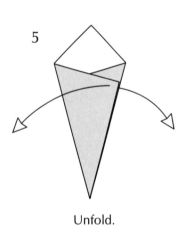

Unfold.

6
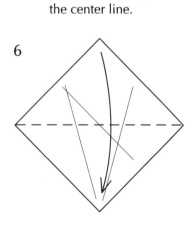

7

Fold the top layer to the dotted lines so it meets the dots.

8

Place your finger between these layers. Let's call this the prehistoric pocket. In step 11 some paper will be folded into it.

**9**

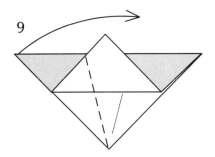

Fold along the crease.

**10**

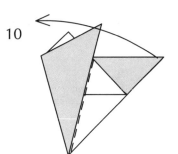

**11**

Tuck inside the prehistoric pocket.

**12**

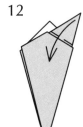

**13**

Unfold.

**14**

Tuck inside.

**15**

Turn over.

**16**

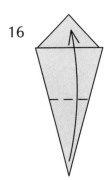

**17**

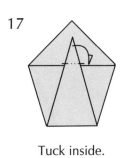

Tuck inside.

**18**

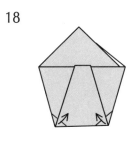

**19**

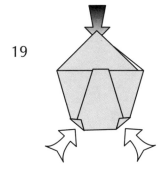

Place your finger all the way inside and squeeze at the bottom. Make the egg round and 3D.

**20**

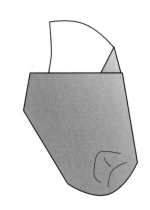

Cracked Dinosaur Egg

# Prehistoric Tree

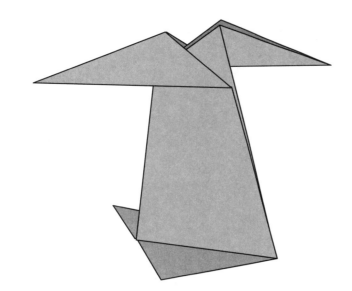

1

Fold and unfold.

2
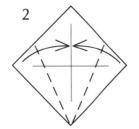
Kite-fold.

3
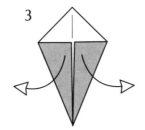
Unfold.

4
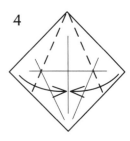
Kite-fold.

5
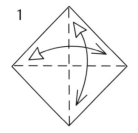
Squash-fold.

6
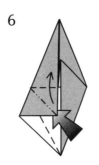
Squash-fold.

7
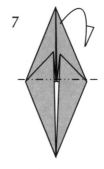
Fold behind.

8
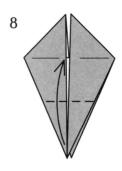
This is the Fish Base.

9
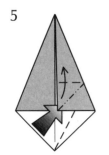
Turn over.

10
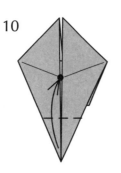
Turn over.

11
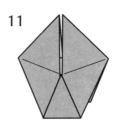

12
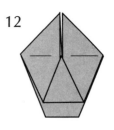
Rotate.

13

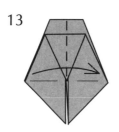

14

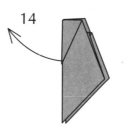

Slide up.

15

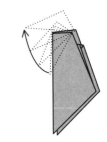

An intermediate step.

16

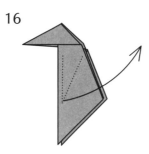

Slide the inside paper up.

17

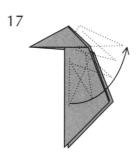

An intermediate step.

18

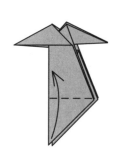

Fold the root up.

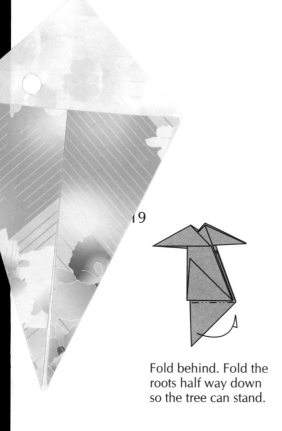

19

Fold behind. Fold the
roots half way down
so the tree can stand.

20

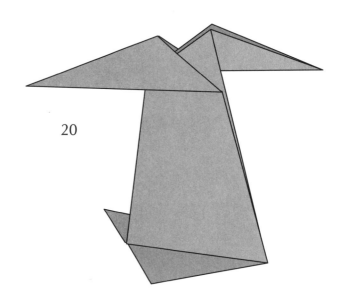

Prehistoric Tree

# Pterodactylus

ter-oh-DAC-til-us

This tiny Jurassic reptile had an 18 inch wing span. It could have actually flapped its wings to fly. It ate insects and fish with its toothed beak. Fossils of Pterodactylus have been found in Europe.

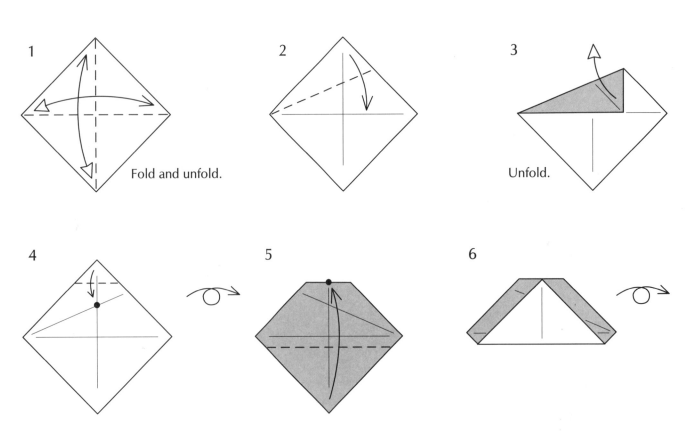

1

Fold and unfold.

2

3

Unfold.

4

5

6

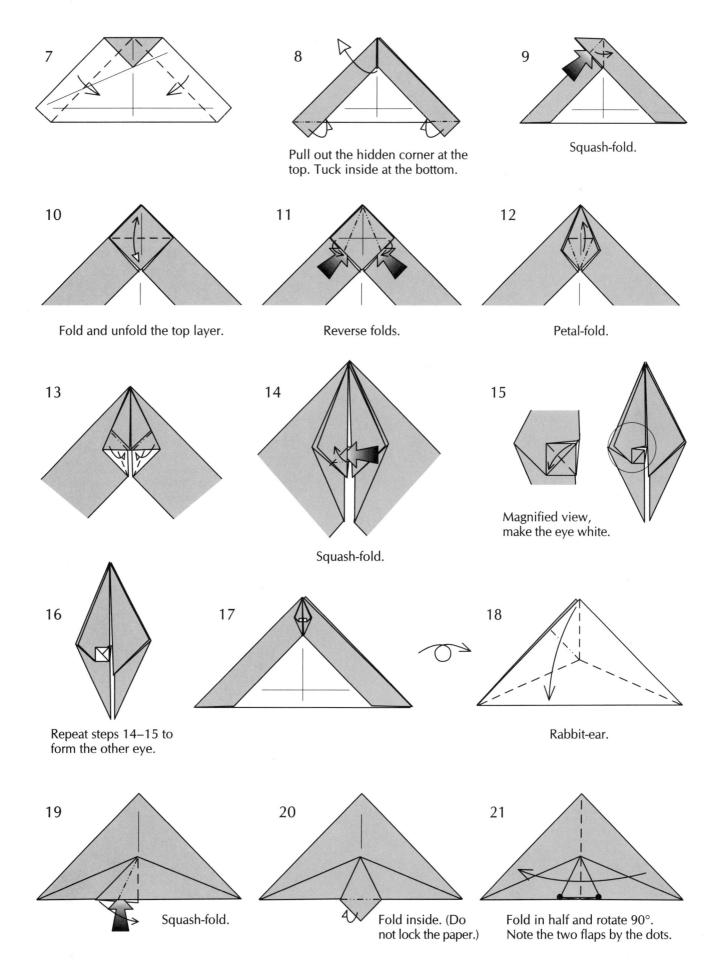

**7**

**8**

Pull out the hidden corner at the top. Tuck inside at the bottom.

**9**

Squash-fold.

**10**

Fold and unfold the top layer.

**11**

Reverse folds.

**12**

Petal-fold.

**13**

**14**

Squash-fold.

**15**

Magnified view, make the eye white.

**16**

Repeat steps 14–15 to form the other eye.

**17**

**18**

Rabbit-ear.

**19**

Squash-fold.

**20**

Fold inside. (Do not lock the paper.)

**21**

Fold in half and rotate 90°. Note the two flaps by the dots.

22

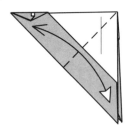

Fold and unfold.

23

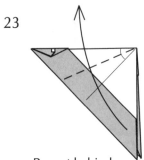

Repeat behind.

24

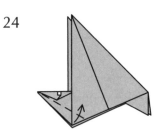

Fold at an angle of one-third, repeat behind.

25

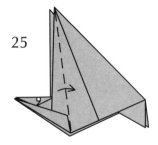

Repeat behind.

26

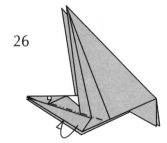

Repeat behind.

27

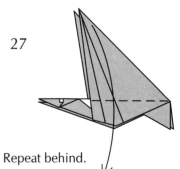

Repeat behind.

28

Repeat behind.

29

Repeat behind.

30

1. Crimp-fold.
2. Rabbit-ear,
   repeat behind.

31

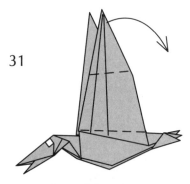

Spread the wings.
Repeat behind.

32

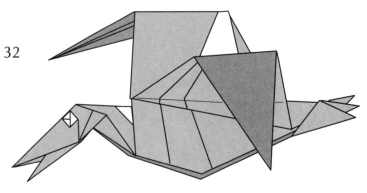

Pterodactylus

# Quetzalcoatlus

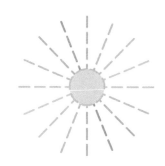

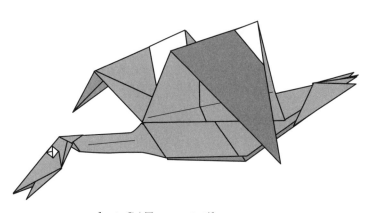

ket-SAT-co-at-til-us

Named for the Aztec God who was represented by a feathered serpent, this was the largest gliding reptile ever discovered. It had a 40 foot wing span. Because of its hollow bones, it was light enough to soar over Cretaceous seas for fish. Fossils were found in Texas.

1

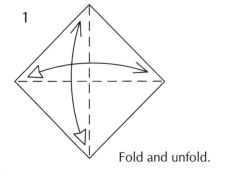

Fold and unfold.

2

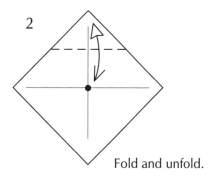

Fold and unfold.

3

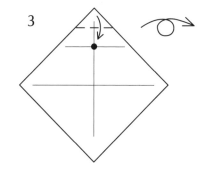

4

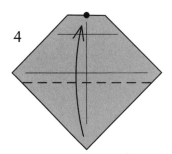

Continue with steps 5–23 of Pterodactylus (page 18).

5

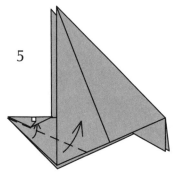

Tuck under the head.
Repeat behind.

6

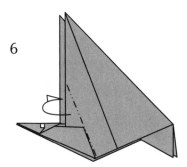

Repeat behind.

7

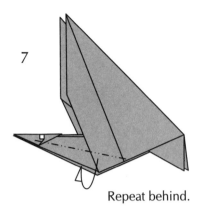

Repeat behind.

8

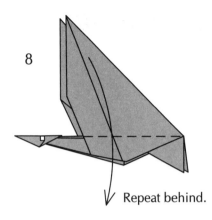

Repeat behind.

9

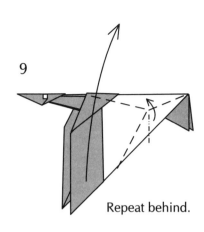

Repeat behind.

10

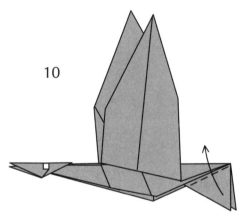

Repeat behind.

11

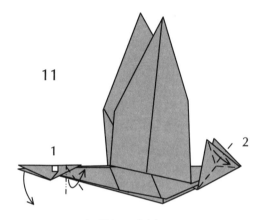

1. Crimp-fold.
2. Rabbit-ear,
   repeat behind.

12

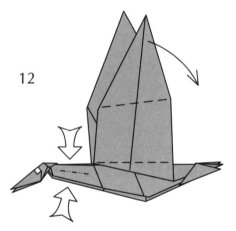

Thin the neck and spread
the wings. Repeat behind.

13

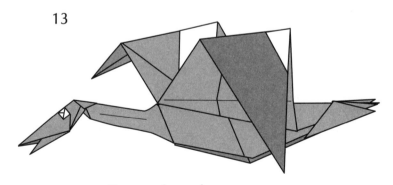

Quetzalcoatlus

# Pteranodon

ter-RAN-oh-don

With a 20 foot wing span, this gliding reptile swooped over Cretaceous seas picking up fish to eat. Its name means "toothless wing". The skin stretching across its "wings" was probably covered with hair. It glided off ocean cliffs in the western U.S.

**1**

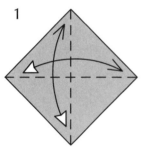

Fold and unfold along the diagonals.

**2**

Kite-fold.

**3**

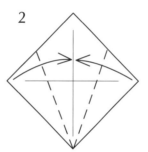

Unfold.

**4**

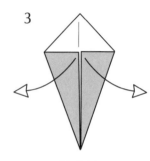

**5**

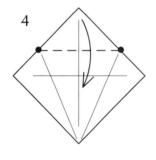

**6**

**7**

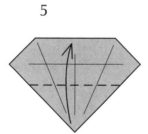

**8**

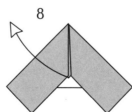

Pull out the hidden corner.

**9**

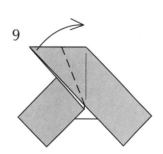

**10**

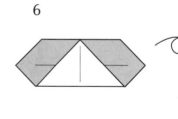

Unfold.

**11**

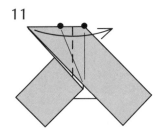

Fold so that
the dots meet.

**12**

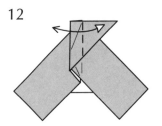

Fold and unfold.

**13**

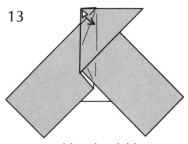

Fold and unfold.

**14**

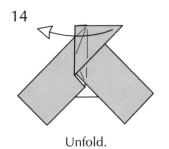

Unfold.

**15**

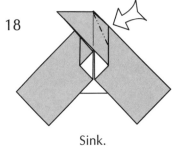

Squash-fold.

**16**

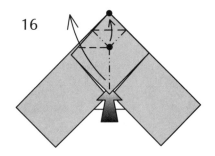

This is similar to a petal
fold. The dots will meet.

**17**

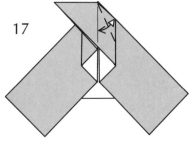

Fold along the crease
line and unfold.

**18**

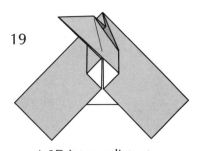

Sink.

**19**

A 3D intermediate step.

**20**

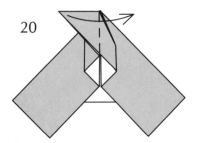

**21**

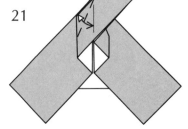

Repeat steps 17–19
on the left.

**22**

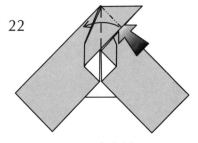

Squash-fold.

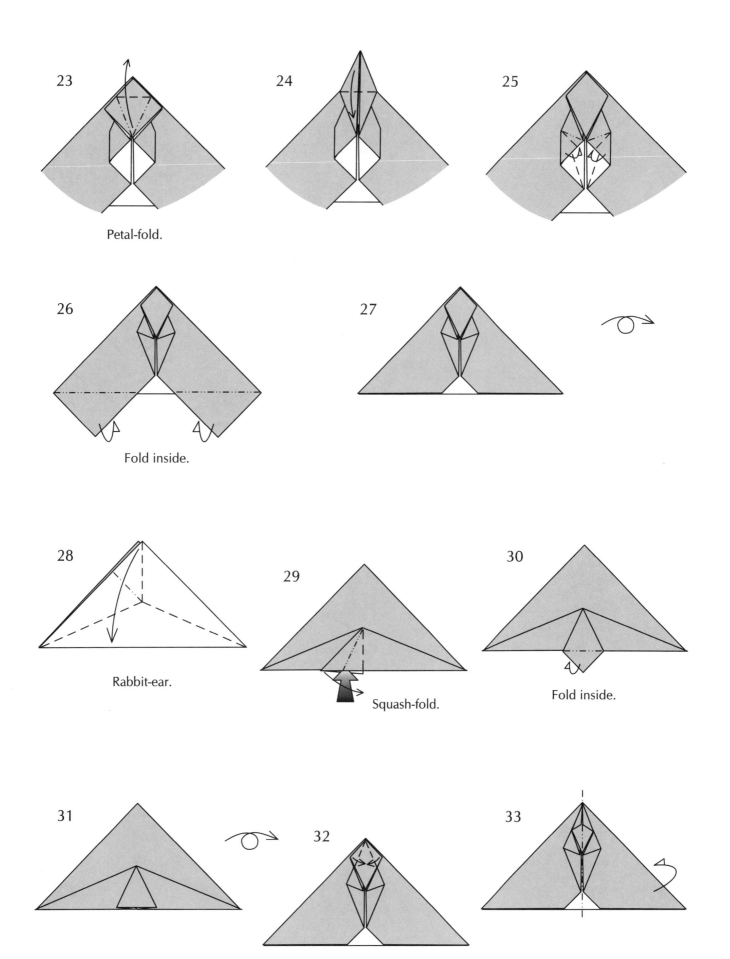

23

24

25

Petal-fold.

26

27

Fold inside.

28

Rabbit-ear.

29

Squash-fold.

30

Fold inside.

31

32

33

34

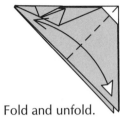

Fold and unfold.

35

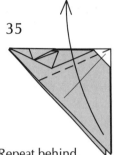

Repeat behind.

36

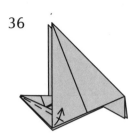

Fold at an angle of one-third,
repeat behind.

37

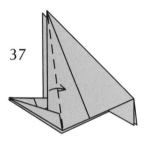

Repeat behind.

38

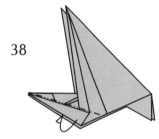

Repeat behind.

39

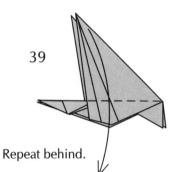

Repeat behind.

40

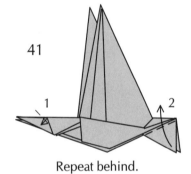

Repeat behind.

41

1    2

Repeat behind.

42

1    2

1. Crimp-fold.
2. Rabbit-ear,
   repeat behind.

43

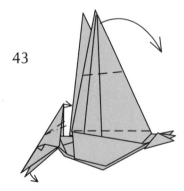

Crimp-fold the crest. Spread the
wings and beak. Repeat behind.

44

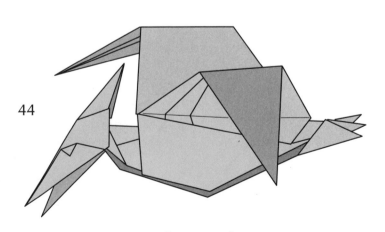

Pteranodon

# Rhamphorynchus

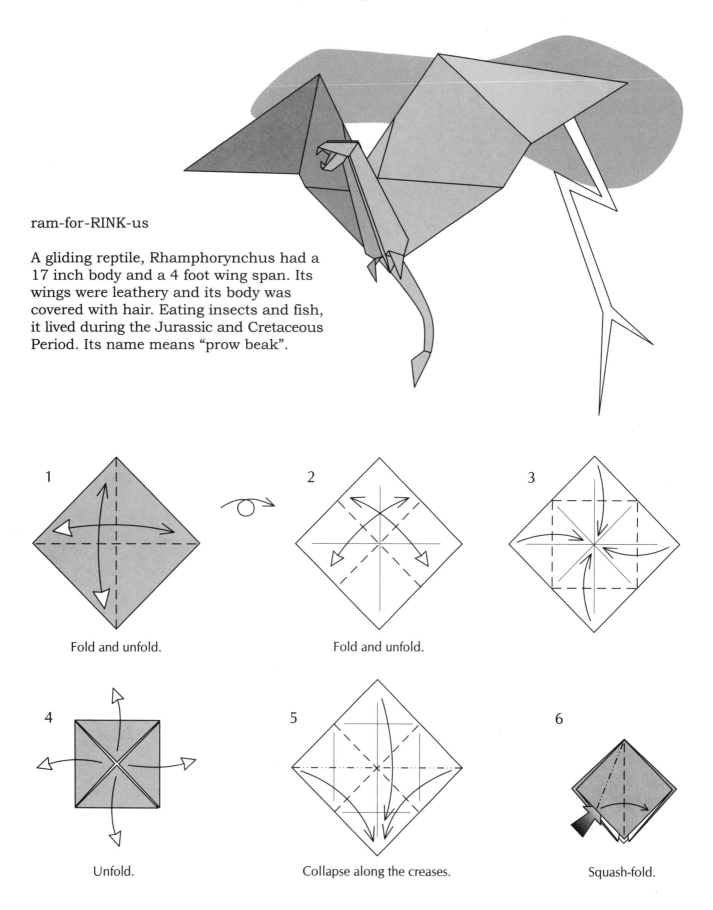

ram-for-RINK-us

A gliding reptile, Rhamphorynchus had a 17 inch body and a 4 foot wing span. Its wings were leathery and its body was covered with hair. Eating insects and fish, it lived during the Jurassic and Cretaceous Period. Its name means "prow beak".

1

Fold and unfold.

2

Fold and unfold.

3

4

Unfold.

5

Collapse along the creases.

6

Squash-fold.

7

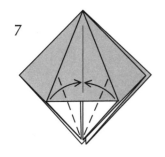

8

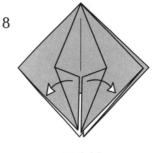

Unfold.

9

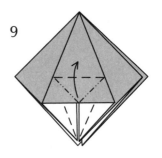

Petal-fold.

10

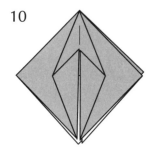

11

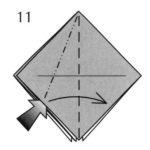

Repeat steps 6–9.

12

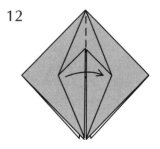

Repeat behind.

13

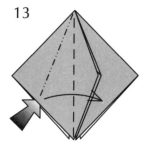

Repeat steps 6–9 in front and behind.

14

This is the Frog Base.

15

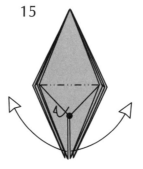

Spread to fold the dot inside.

16

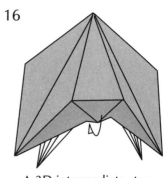

A 3D intermediate step.

17

Repeat steps 14–16 three more times on the back and sides.

18

19

Unfold.

20

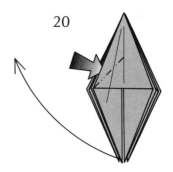

Reverse-fold.

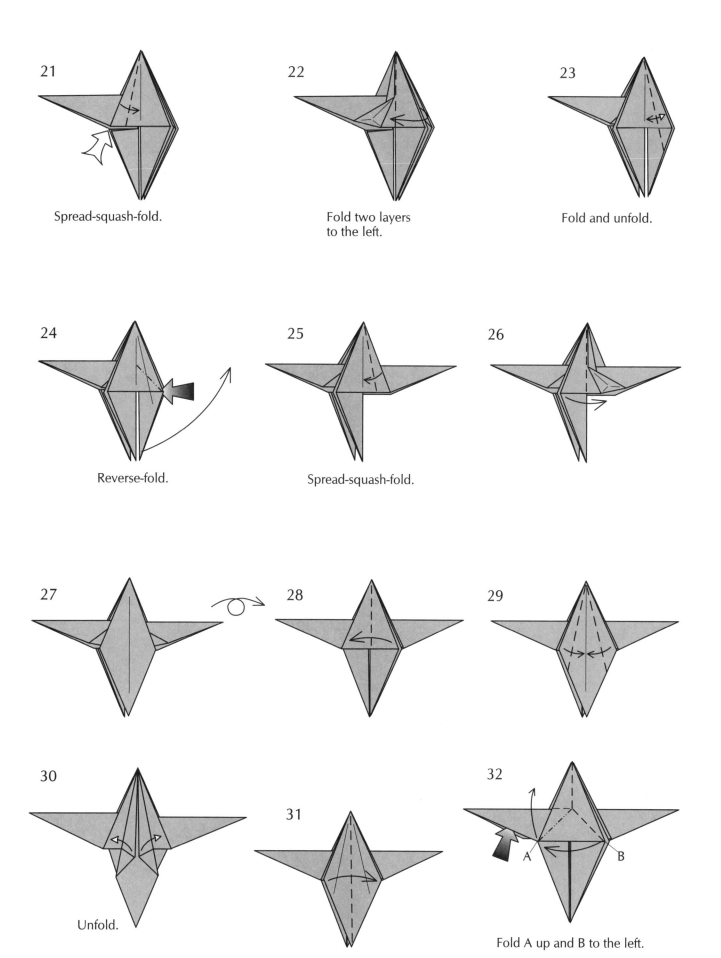

21

Spread-squash-fold.

22

Fold two layers
to the left.

23

Fold and unfold.

24

Reverse-fold.

25

Spread-squash-fold.

26

27

28

29

30

Unfold.

31

32

Fold A up and B to the left.

A          B

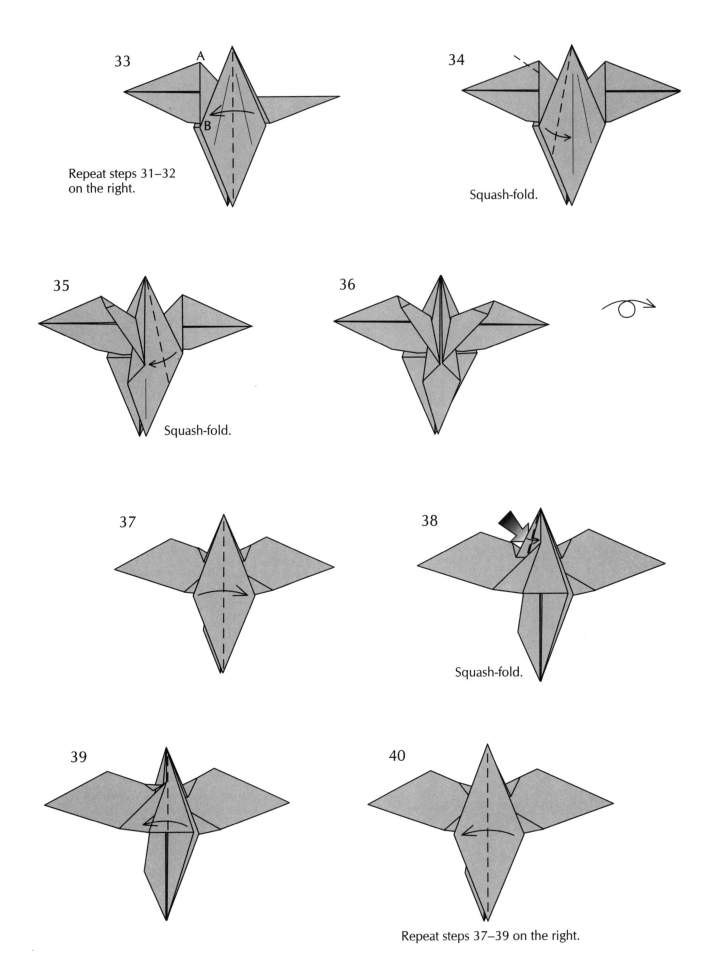

33

A

B

Repeat steps 31–32
on the right.

34

Squash-fold.

35

Squash-fold.

36

37

38

Squash-fold.

39

40

Repeat steps 37–39 on the right.

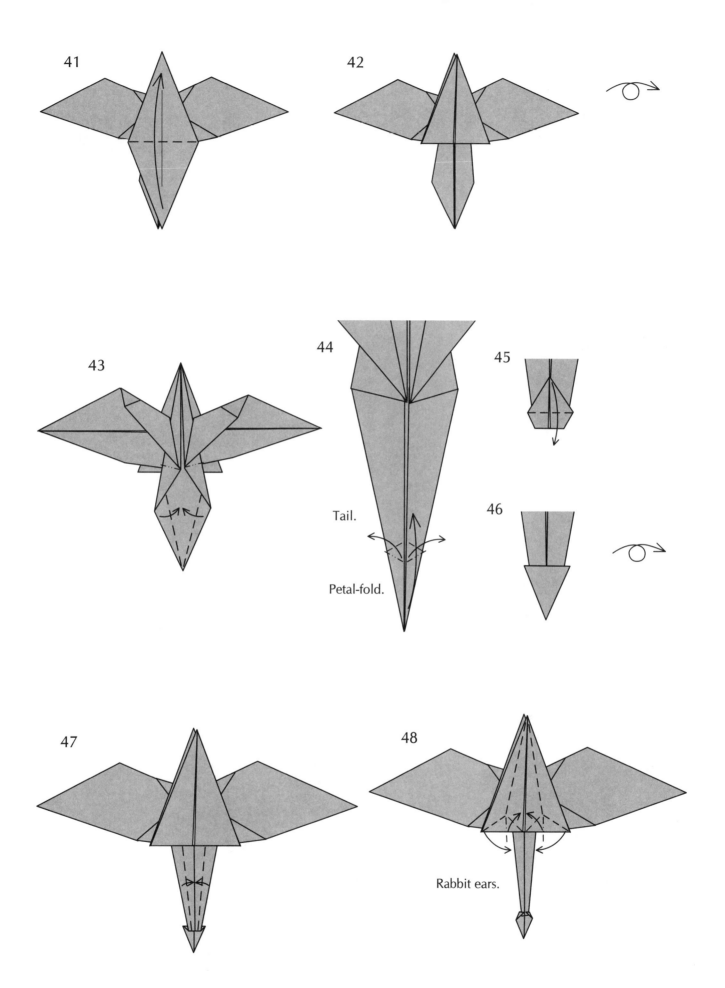

41

42

43

44

Tail.

Petal-fold.

45

46

47

48

Rabbit ears.

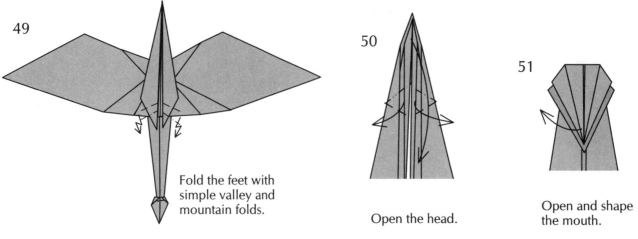

49

Fold the feet with simple valley and mountain folds.

50

Open the head.

51

Open and shape the mouth.

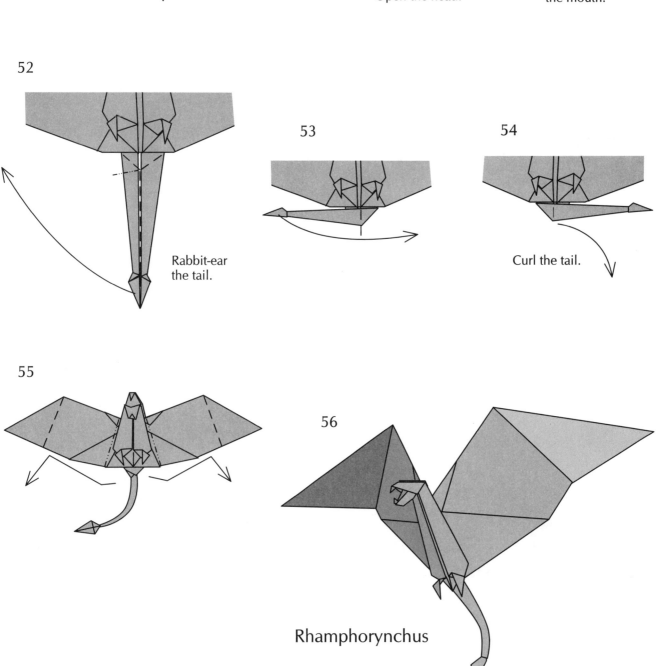

52

Rabbit-ear the tail.

53

54

Curl the tail.

55

56

Rhamphorynchus

# Elasmosaurus

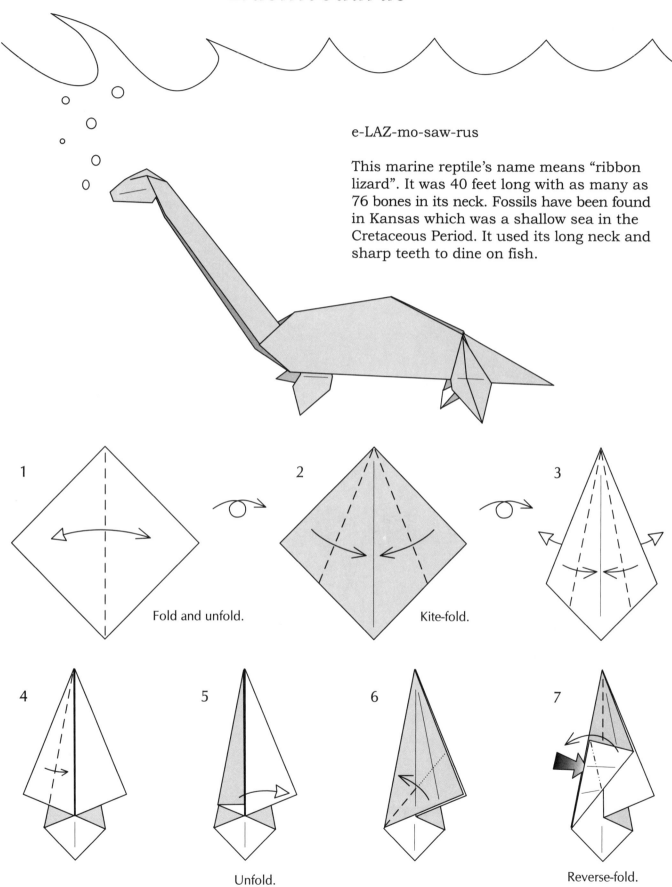

e-LAZ-mo-saw-rus

This marine reptile's name means "ribbon lizard". It was 40 feet long with as many as 76 bones in its neck. Fossils have been found in Kansas which was a shallow sea in the Cretaceous Period. It used its long neck and sharp teeth to dine on fish.

1

Fold and unfold.

2

Kite-fold.

3

4

5

Unfold.

6

7

Reverse-fold.

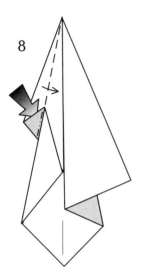

8

Reverse-fold.

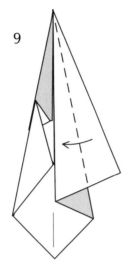

9

Repeat steps 4–8
on the right.

10

Only part of the model
is drawn. Make a thin
squash fold.

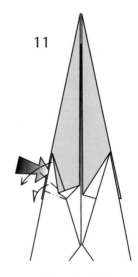

11

Squash-fold.

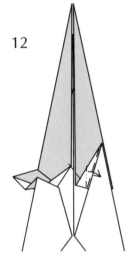

12

Repeat steps 9–10
on the right.

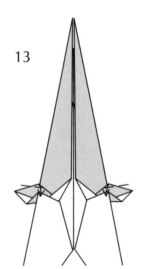

13

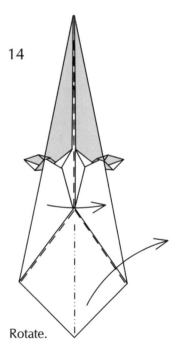

14

Rotate.

15

Reverse-fold on the left.
Double-rabbit-ear on the right.

16

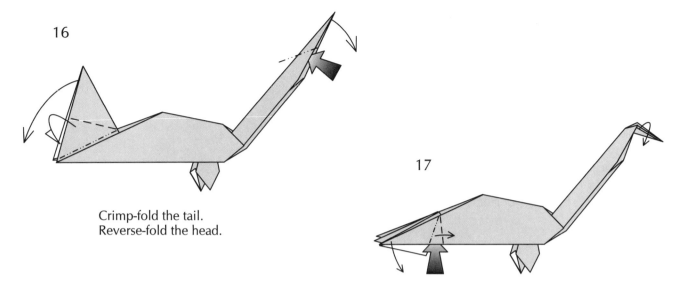

Crimp-fold the tail.
Reverse-fold the head.

17

Crimp-fold the tail. Fold down one of
the layers at the head. Repeat behind.

18

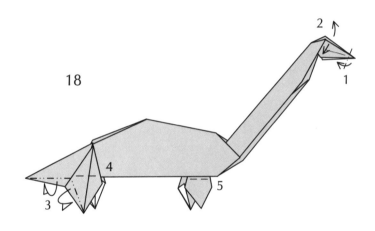

1. Reverse-fold.
2. Spread and open the head.
3. Fold the back feet and tail.
4 and 5. Bend the feet.
Repeat behind.

19

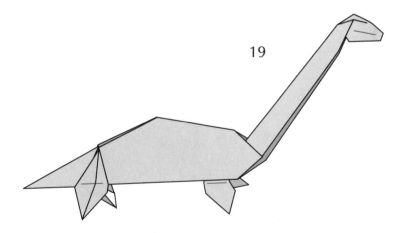

Elasmosaurus

# Tanystropheus

tan-e-STRO-fee-us

This lizard lived on the shores of Triassic seas in
Germany. The hip structure clearly prevents it from
being called a dinosaur. Its 9 foot long neck was more
than half its total 15 foot length. It could remain on the
shore and fish for food beneath the surface of the water.

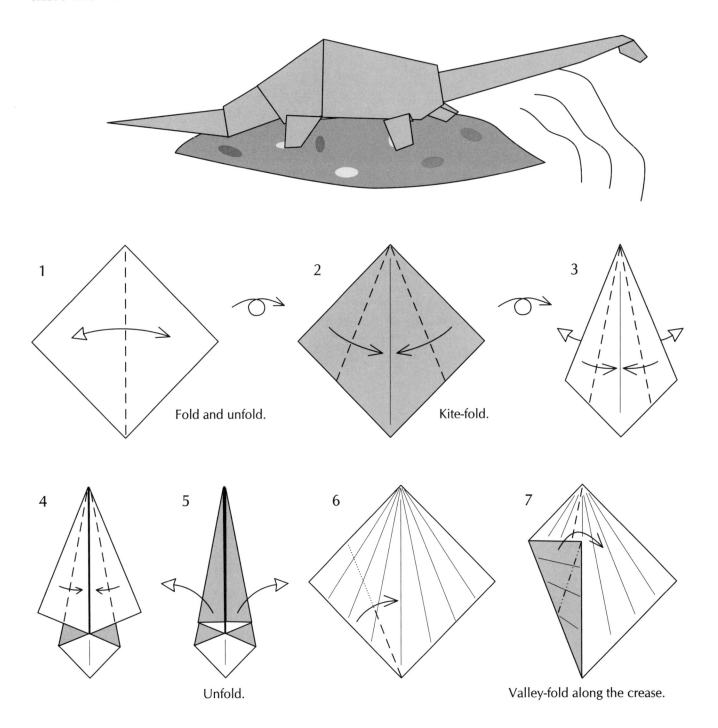

1

2 Fold and unfold.

Kite-fold.

4

5 Unfold.

6

7 Valley-fold along the crease.

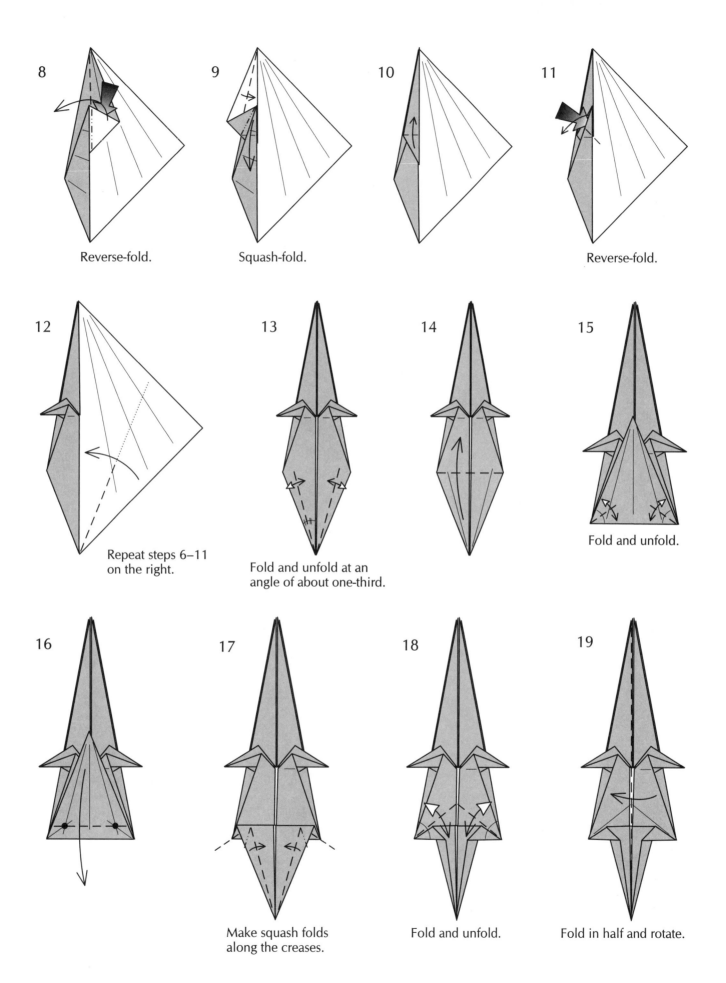

**8** Reverse-fold.

**9** Squash-fold.

**10**

**11** Reverse-fold.

**12** Repeat steps 6–11 on the right.

**13** Fold and unfold at an angle of about one-third.

**14**

**15** Fold and unfold.

**16**

**17** Make squash folds along the creases.

**18** Fold and unfold.

**19** Fold in half and rotate.

**20**

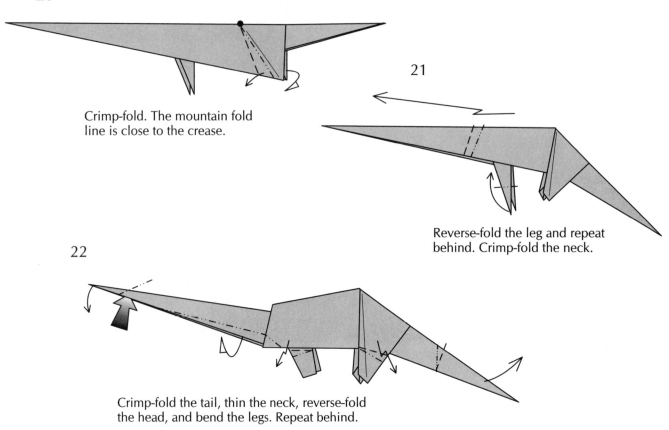

Crimp-fold. The mountain fold
line is close to the crease.

**21**

Reverse-fold the leg and repeat
behind. Crimp-fold the neck.

**22**

Crimp-fold the tail, thin the neck, reverse-fold
the head, and bend the legs. Repeat behind.

**23**

The head is drawn. Fold down one of
the layers at the head. Repeat behind.

**24**

Reverse-fold.

**25**

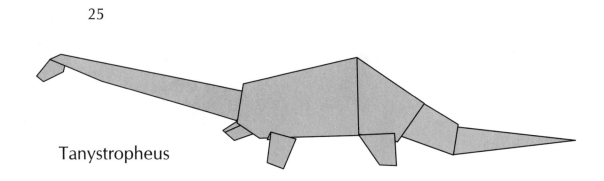

Tanystropheus

# Riojasaurus

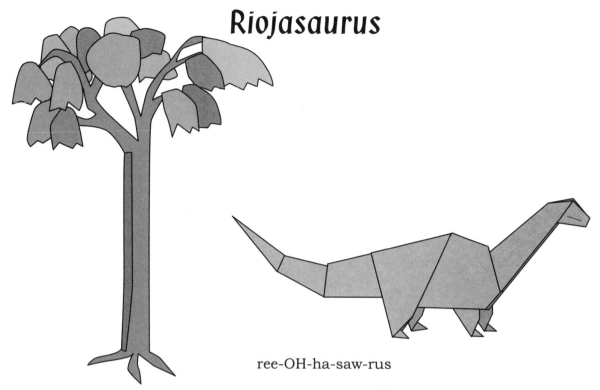

ree-OH-ha-saw-rus

This plant eating dinosaur lived at the end of the Triassic Period. It was 30 feet long and kept its four elephant-like legs on the the ground all the time. It is named for La Rioja Provence in Argentina where its fossils were found. It was a relative of the later, larger sauropods.

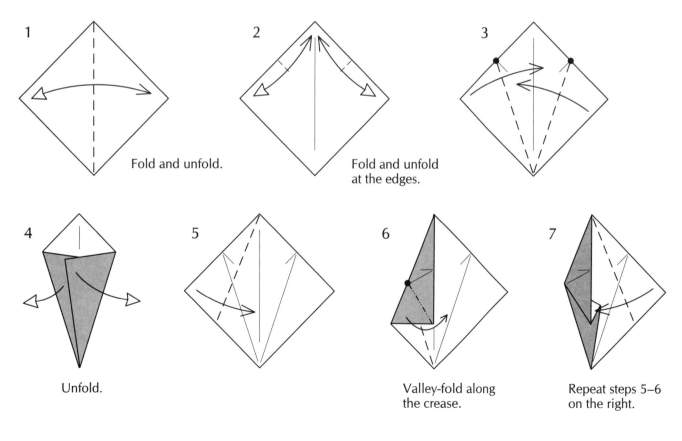

1

Fold and unfold.

2

Fold and unfold at the edges.

3

4

Unfold.

5

6

Valley-fold along the crease.

7

Repeat steps 5–6 on the right.

8

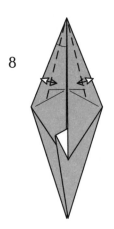

Fold and unfold at an
angle of one-third.

9

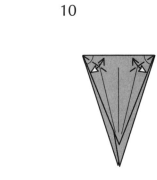

10

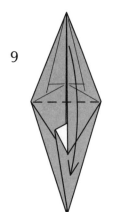

Fold and unfold
the top layer.

11

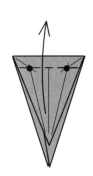

12

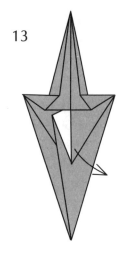

Valley-fold along
the creases for the
squash folds.

13

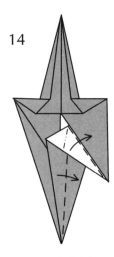

Slide out the paper.

14

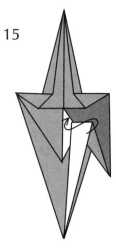

Squash-fold.

15

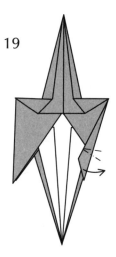

Tuck under the
dark paper.

16

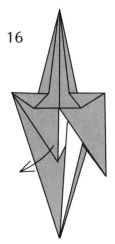

Repeat steps
13–15 on the left.

17

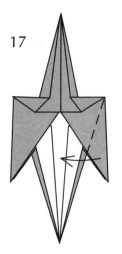

18

19

Squash-fold.

40    *Dinosaur Origami*

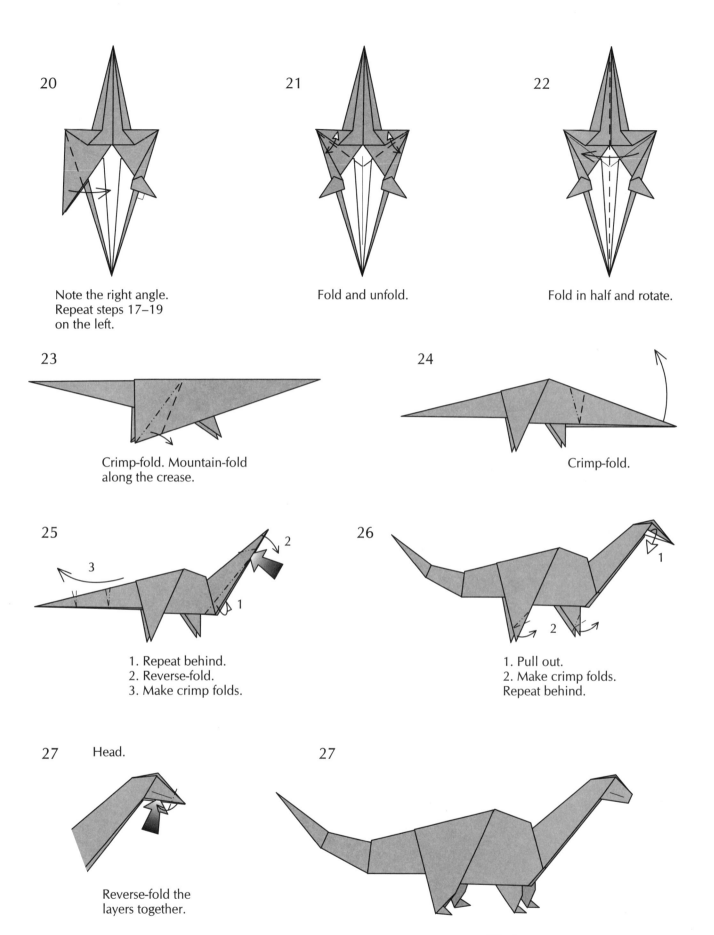

**20**

Note the right angle. Repeat steps 17–19 on the left.

**21**

Fold and unfold.

**22**

Fold in half and rotate.

**23**

Crimp-fold. Mountain-fold along the crease.

**24**

Crimp-fold.

**25**

1. Repeat behind.
2. Reverse-fold.
3. Make crimp folds.

**26**

1. Pull out.
2. Make crimp folds.
Repeat behind.

**27** Head.

Reverse-fold the layers together.

**27**

Riojasaurus

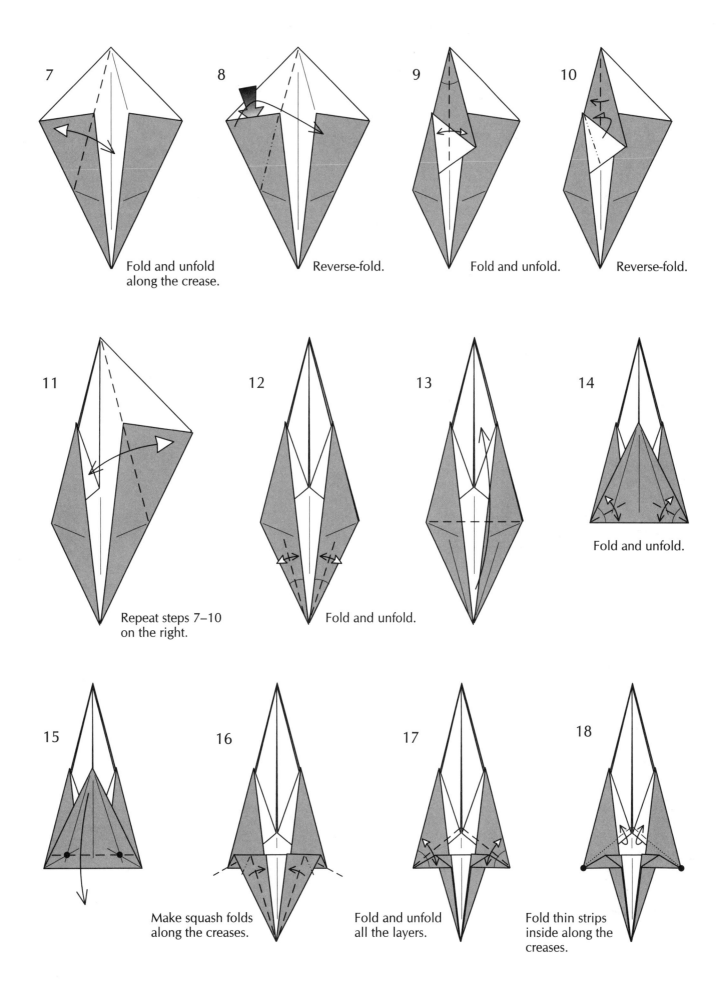

**7** Fold and unfold along the crease.

**8** Reverse-fold.

**9** Fold and unfold.

**10** Reverse-fold.

**11** Repeat steps 7–10 on the right.

**12** Fold and unfold.

**13**

**14** Fold and unfold.

**15**

**16** Make squash folds along the creases.

**17** Fold and unfold all the layers.

**18** Fold thin strips inside along the creases.

*Apatosaurus* 43

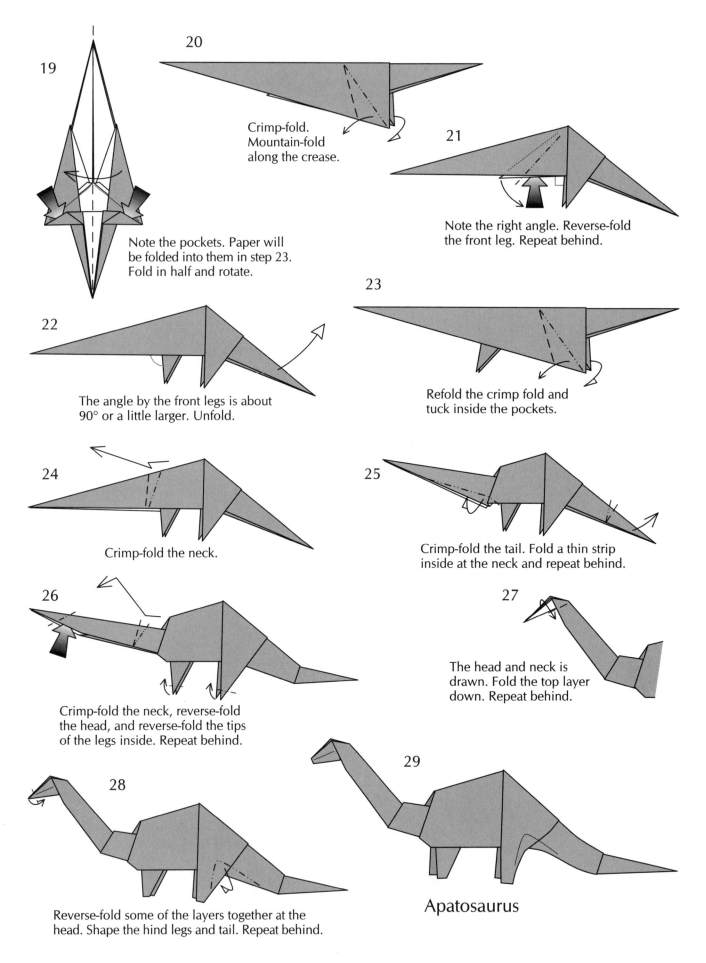

**19**

Note the pockets. Paper will be folded into them in step 23. Fold in half and rotate.

**20**

Crimp-fold. Mountain-fold along the crease.

**21**

Note the right angle. Reverse-fold the front leg. Repeat behind.

**22**

The angle by the front legs is about 90° or a little larger. Unfold.

**23**

Refold the crimp fold and tuck inside the pockets.

**24**

Crimp-fold the neck.

**25**

Crimp-fold the tail. Fold a thin strip inside at the neck and repeat behind.

**26**

Crimp-fold the neck, reverse-fold the head, and reverse-fold the tips of the legs inside. Repeat behind.

**27**

The head and neck is drawn. Fold the top layer down. Repeat behind.

**28**

Reverse-fold some of the layers together at the head. Shape the hind legs and tail. Repeat behind.

**29**

Apatosaurus

# Brachiosaurus

BRAKE-ee-oh-saw-rus

This 75 foot long Jurassic dinosaur was called "arm lizard" because its front legs were longer than its back legs. The placement of the nose on top of its head was once thought to aid in breathing when submerged in deep water. Now some paleontologists believe it lived on high ground, eating pine needles, since the skeleton could not have withstood the pressure of deep water. Fossils were found in Colorado.

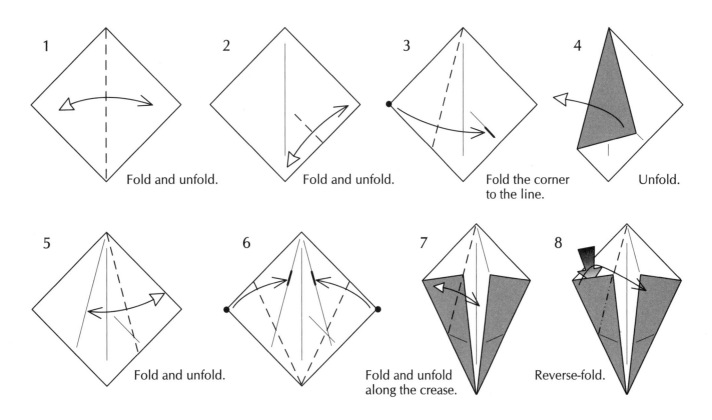

1. Fold and unfold.

2. Fold and unfold.

3. Fold the corner to the line.

4. Unfold.

5. Fold and unfold.

6. Fold and unfold along the crease.

7.

8. Reverse-fold.

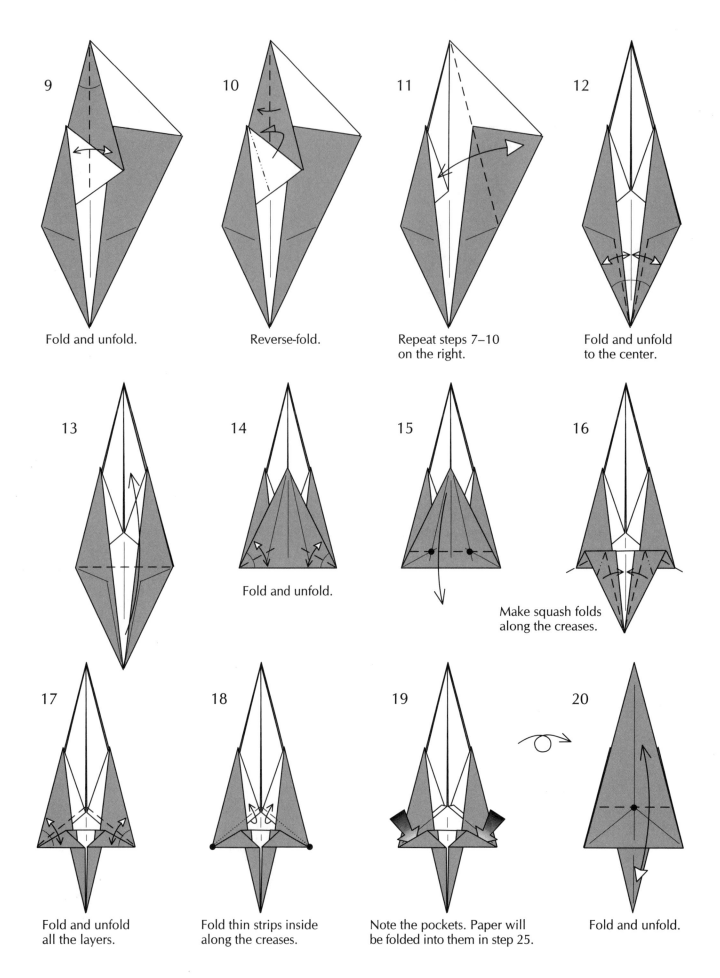

**9** Fold and unfold.

**10** Reverse-fold.

**11** Repeat steps 7–10 on the right.

**12** Fold and unfold to the center.

**13**

**14** Fold and unfold.

**15**

**16** Make squash folds along the creases.

**17** Fold and unfold all the layers.

**18** Fold thin strips inside along the creases.

**19** Note the pockets. Paper will be folded into them in step 25.

**20** Fold and unfold.

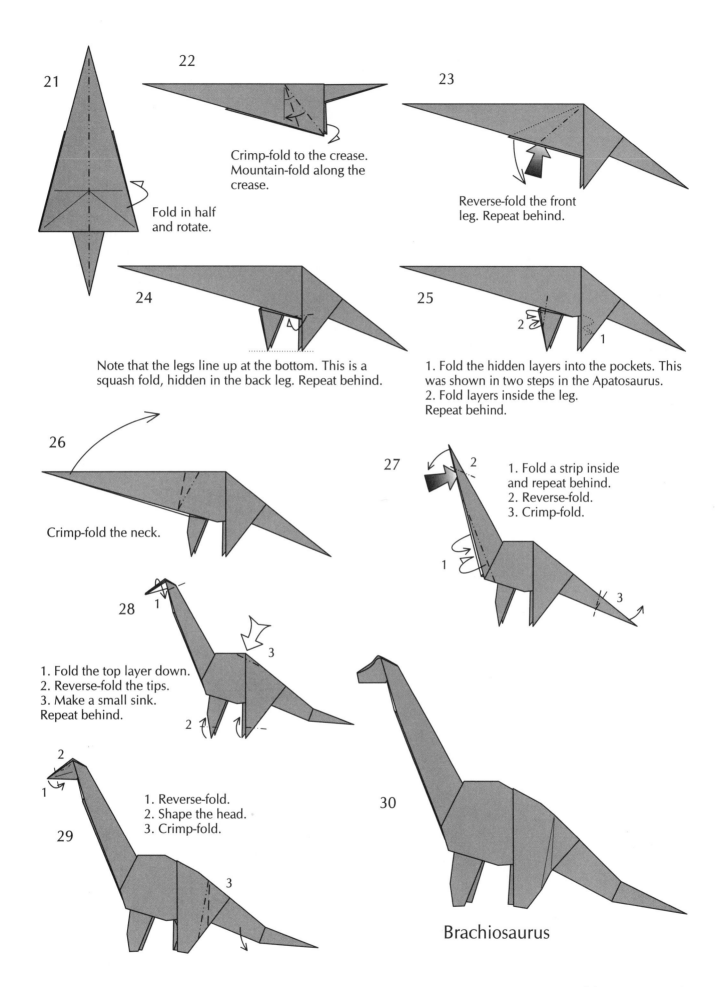

21

22 Crimp-fold to the crease.
Mountain-fold along the
crease.

Fold in half
and rotate.

23 Reverse-fold the front
leg. Repeat behind.

24 Note that the legs line up at the bottom. This is a
squash fold, hidden in the back leg. Repeat behind.

25 1. Fold the hidden layers into the pockets. This
was shown in two steps in the Apatosaurus.
2. Fold layers inside the leg.
Repeat behind.

26 Crimp-fold the neck.

27 1. Fold a strip inside
and repeat behind.
2. Reverse-fold.
3. Crimp-fold.

28 1. Fold the top layer down.
2. Reverse-fold the tips.
3. Make a small sink.
Repeat behind.

29 1. Reverse-fold.
2. Shape the head.
3. Crimp-fold.

30

Brachiosaurus

# Diplodocus

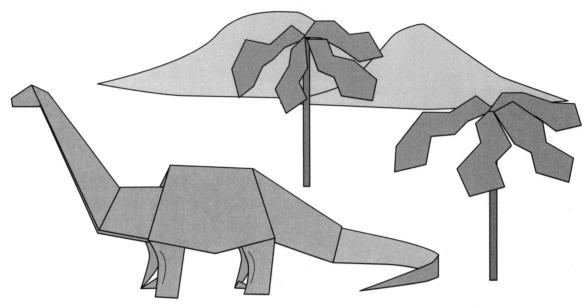

dih-PLOD-u kus

One of the longest dinosaurs ever found, this Jurassic creature was 90 feet from is head to its tail tip. Its name means "double beam" because of the double "Y" shaped vertebrae in its tail. This provided for more place for muscle attachments and made the tail a whip-like weapon. Fossils were found in the Rocky Mountain States.

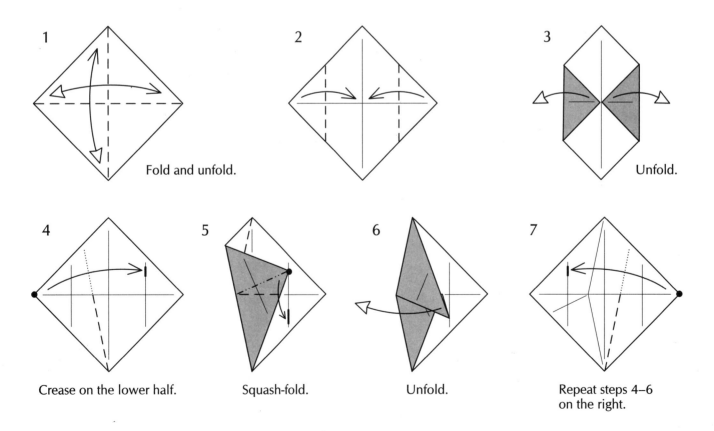

1

Fold and unfold.

2

3

Unfold.

4

Crease on the lower half.

5

Squash-fold.

6

Unfold.

7

Repeat steps 4–6 on the right.

8

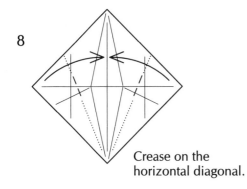

Crease on the
horizontal diagonal.

9

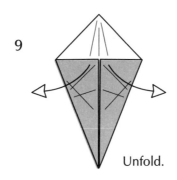

Unfold.

10

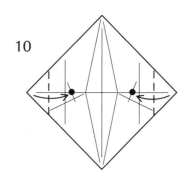

11

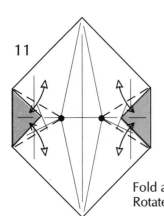

12

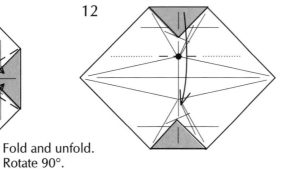

Fold and unfold.
Rotate 90°.

13

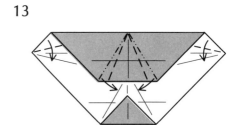

Mountain-fold along the
creases for these squash folds.

14

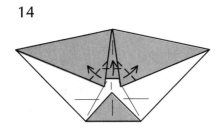

Spread the paper.

15

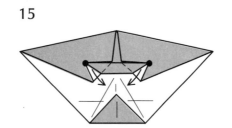

Note the horizontal
line between the dots.

16

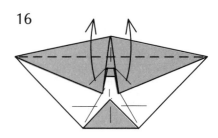

17

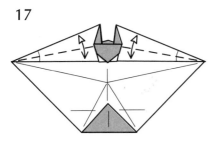

Fold and unfold the top layers to
bisect the angles. Rotate 180°.

18

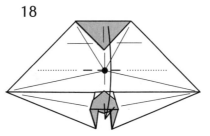

Repeat steps 12–17.

19

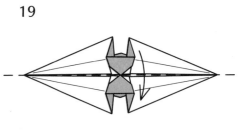

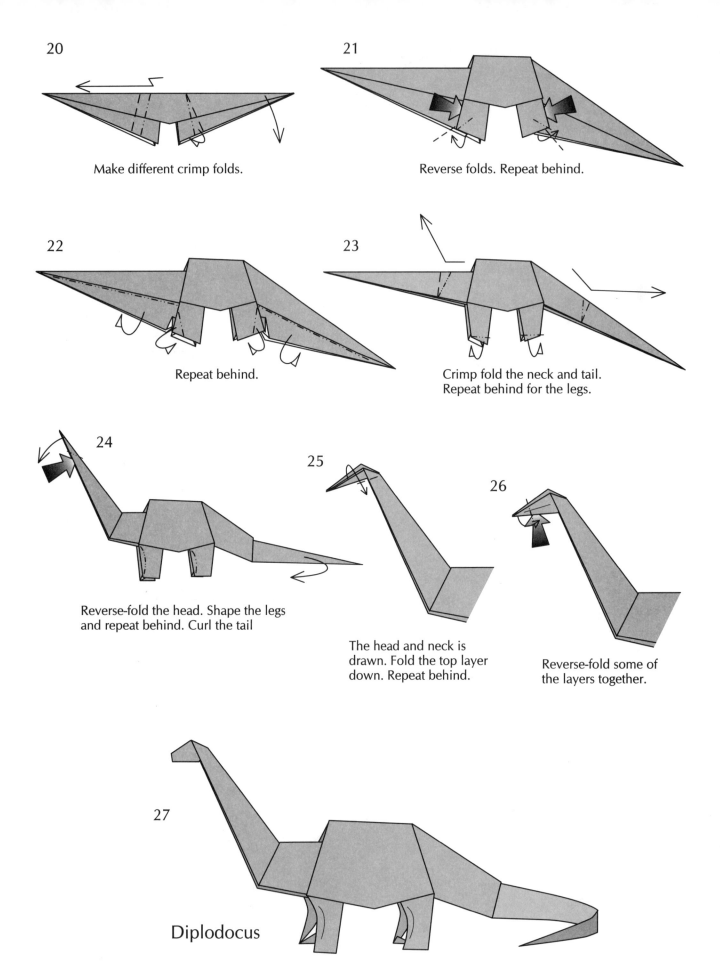

20

Make different crimp folds.

21

Reverse folds. Repeat behind.

22

Repeat behind.

23

Crimp fold the neck and tail.
Repeat behind for the legs.

24

Reverse-fold the head. Shape the legs
and repeat behind. Curl the tail

25

The head and neck is
drawn. Fold the top layer
down. Repeat behind.

26

Reverse-fold some of
the layers together.

27

Diplodocus

# Dimetrodon

di-ME-tro-don

This was a very powerful meat eating reptile. Its name means "double measure tooth" because of its many knife-like teeth. It lived in the Permian Period immediately preceding the Mesozoic Era. It was about 10 feet long and the "sail" on its back helped regulate its body temperature.

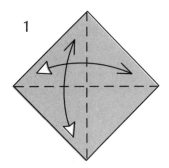

1

Fold and unfold.

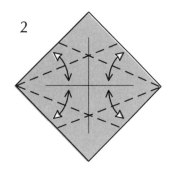

2

Kite-fold and unfold.

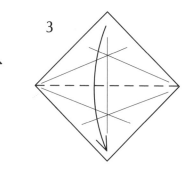

3

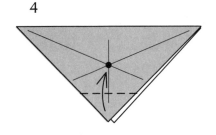

4

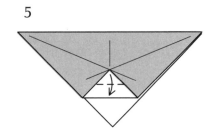

5

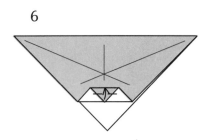

6

**7**

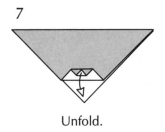

Unfold.

**8**

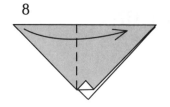

**9**

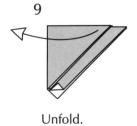

Unfold.

**10**

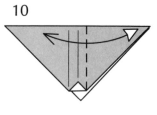

Fold to the left
and unfold.

**11**

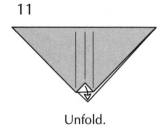

Unfold.

**12**

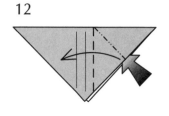

Squash fold.

**13**

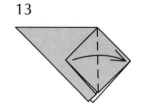

**14**

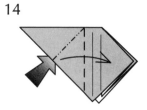

Repeat steps
12–13 on the left.

**15**

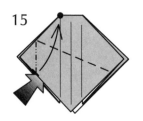

Squash fold.

**16**

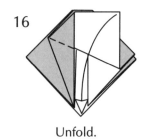

Unfold.

**17**

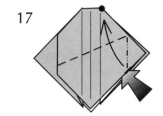

Repeat steps 15–16
three more times on
the right and back.

**18**

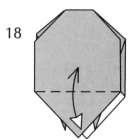

Fold up and unfold.
Repeat behind.

**19**

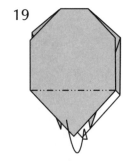

Mountain-fold along the
crease. Repeat behind.

**20**

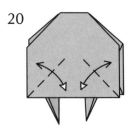

Fold and unfold.
Repeat behind.

**21**

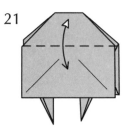

Fold down
and unfold.

**22**

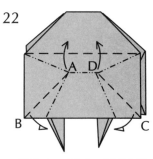

This is a tricky fold! Lift
A–D up while bringing
B and C closer together.

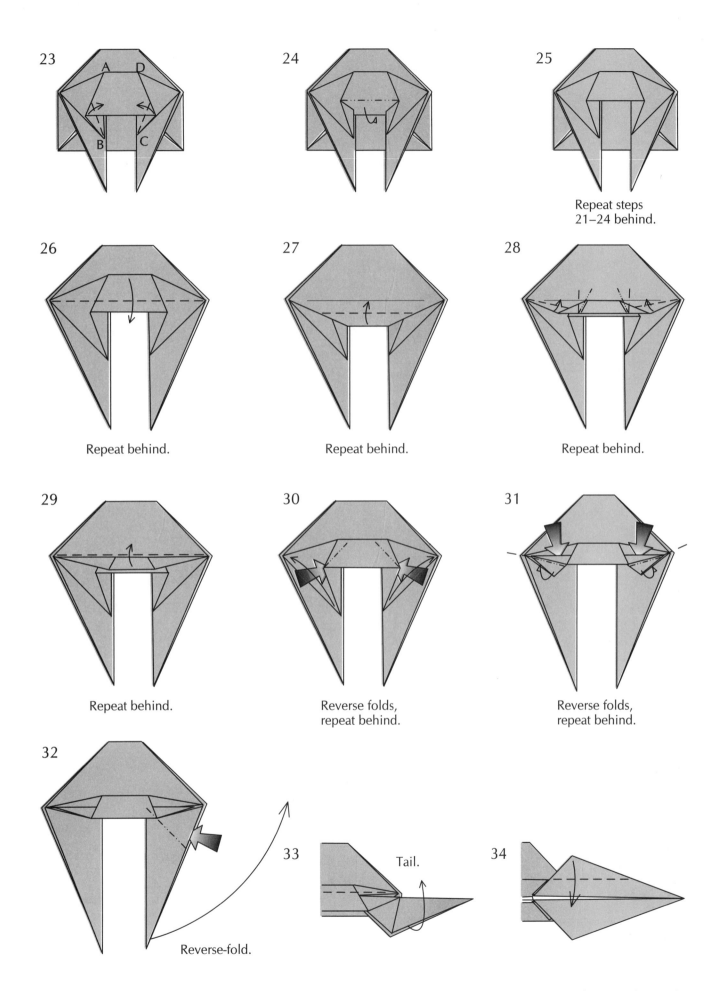

23

24

25

Repeat steps
21–24 behind.

26

Repeat behind.

27

Repeat behind.

28

Repeat behind.

29

Repeat behind.

30

Reverse folds,
repeat behind.

31

Reverse folds,
repeat behind.

32

Reverse-fold.

33

Tail.

34

*Dimetrodon* 53

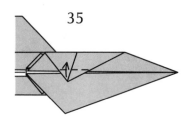

35

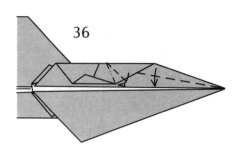

36

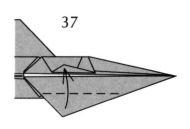

37

Repeat steps 34–36.

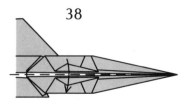

38

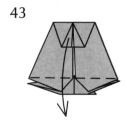

39

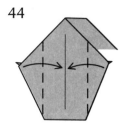

40

Head.

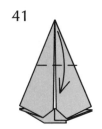

41

42

43

44

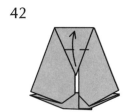

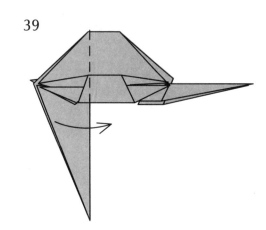

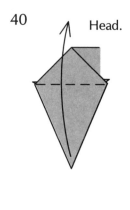

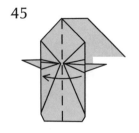

45

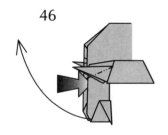

46

Reverse-fold.

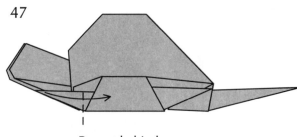

47

Repeat behind.

48

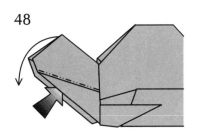

Reverse-fold.

49

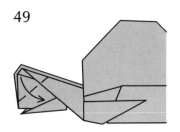

Repeat behind.

50

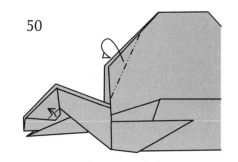

Form the eye and shape
the back. Repeat behind.

51

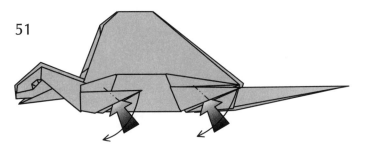

Reverse folds, repeat behind.

52

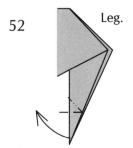

Leg.

Crimp-fold the four legs.

53

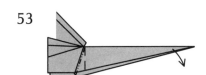

Crimp-fold and curl the tail.

54

Pleat Dimetrodon's sail.

55

Dimetrodon

# Spinosaurus

SPINE-oh-saw-rus

This 40 foot long dinosaur was a fierce meat eater. The sail down its back helped control its body heat. Fossils were found in Egypt. It lived at the end of the Cretaceous Period. Spinosaurus means "spine lizard". Despite the sail, Spinosaurus was not related to Dimetrodon.

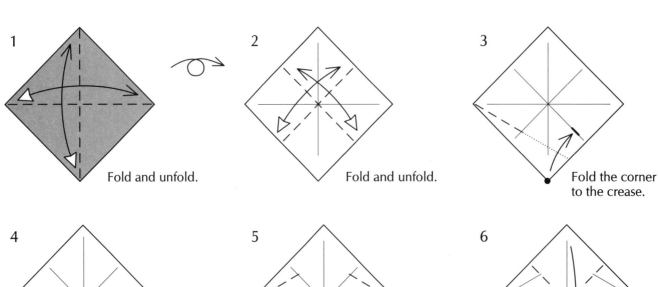

1 Fold and unfold.

2 Fold and unfold.

3 Fold the corner to the crease.

4 Unfold.

5 Repeat steps 3–4 three more times.

6 Collapse along the creases.

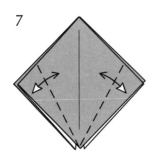

**7**

Fold and unfold along hidden creases. Repeat behind.

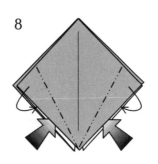

**8**

Reverse folds. Repeat behind.

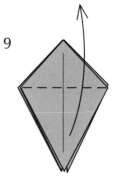

**9**

Repeat behind.

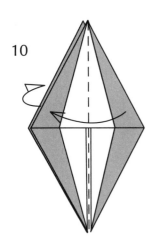

**10**

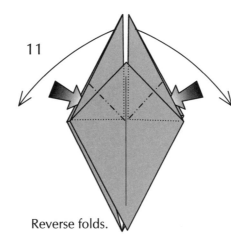

**11**

Reverse folds.

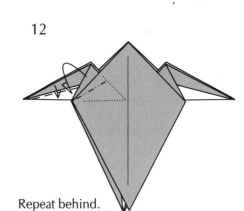

**12**

Repeat behind.

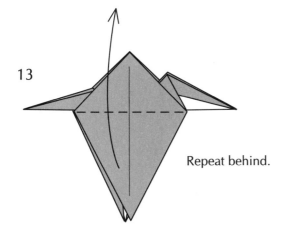

**13**

Repeat behind.

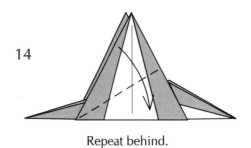

**14**

Repeat behind.

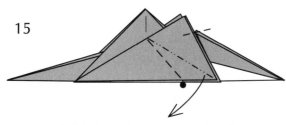

**15**

Squash-fold. The dot is at the color change on a hidden layer. Repeat behind.

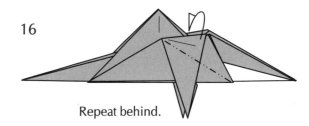

**16**

Repeat behind.

*Spinosaurus* 57

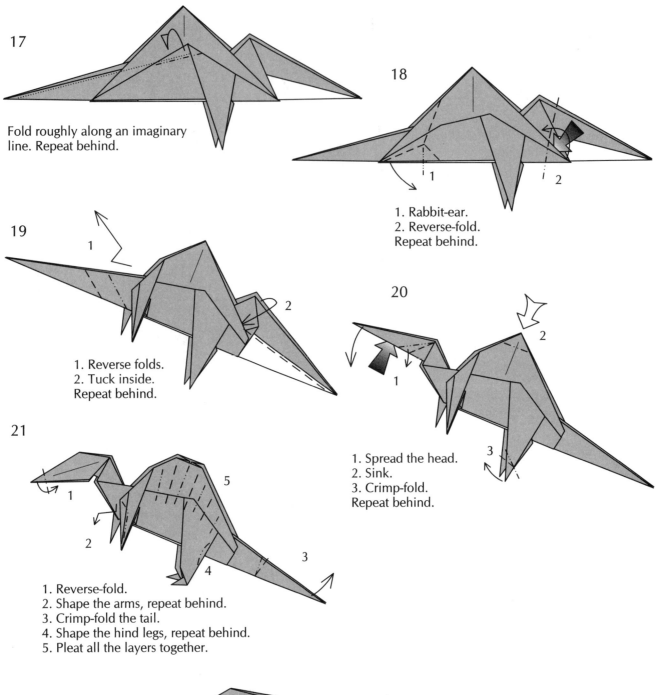

**17**

Fold roughly along an imaginary line. Repeat behind.

**18**

1. Rabbit-ear.
2. Reverse-fold.
Repeat behind.

**19**

1. Reverse folds.
2. Tuck inside.
Repeat behind.

**20**

1. Spread the head.
2. Sink.
3. Crimp-fold.
Repeat behind.

**21**

1. Reverse-fold.
2. Shape the arms, repeat behind.
3. Crimp-fold the tail.
4. Shape the hind legs, repeat behind.
5. Pleat all the layers together.

**22**

Spinosaurus

# Tyrannosaurus

ti-RAN-oh-saw-rus

Probably the largest meat eater ever to walk the earth, this "tyrant lizard" was up to 50 feet long. The 6 inch dagger-like teeth were perfect for eating other Cretaceous animals. Once thought to be feared, some paleontologists now believe it was a scavenger, and could be easily beaten in a fight. Its arms were so small and weak that it probably could not get up if knocked over by the swing of a heavy tail. It used its claws like knives but could not reach its hand to its mouth.

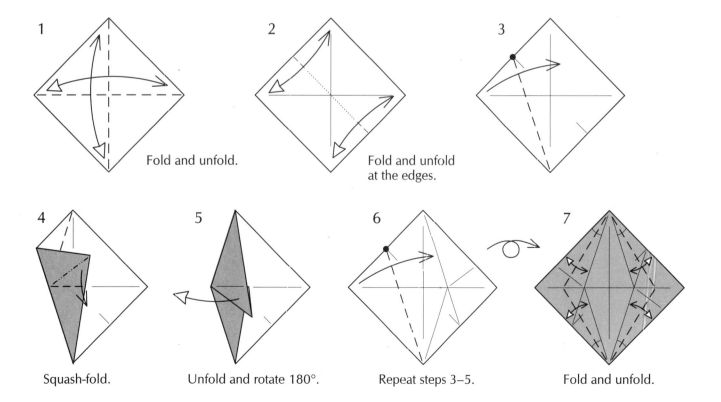

1. Fold and unfold.

2. Fold and unfold at the edges.

3.

4. Squash-fold.

5. Unfold and rotate 180°.

6. Repeat steps 3–5.

7. Fold and unfold.

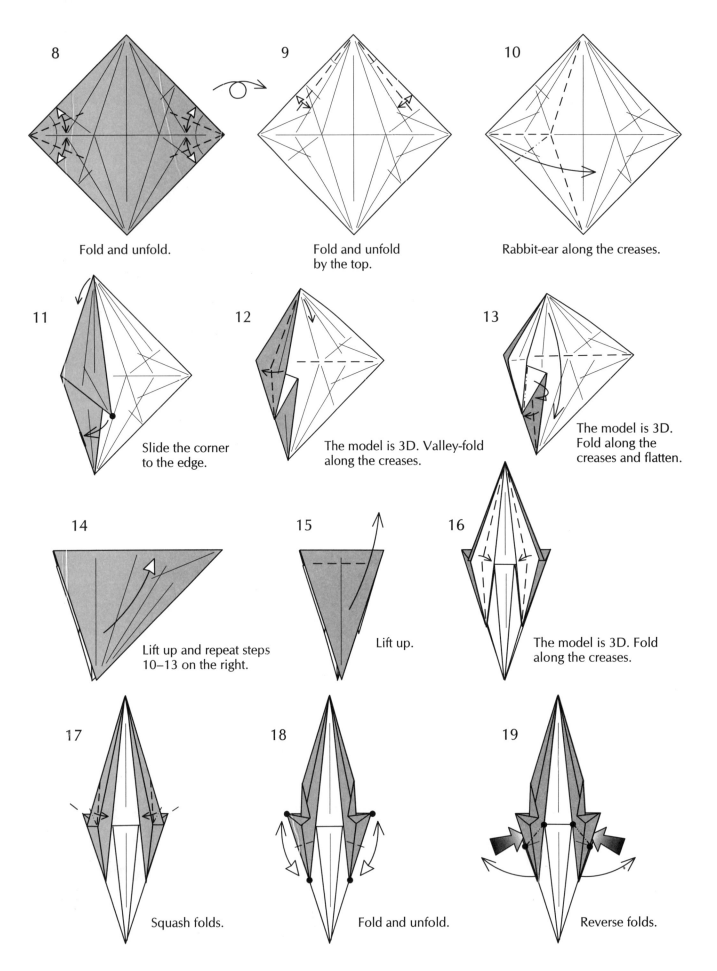

8

Fold and unfold.

9

Fold and unfold
by the top.

10

Rabbit-ear along the creases.

11

Slide the corner
to the edge.

12

The model is 3D. Valley-fold
along the creases.

13

The model is 3D.
Fold along the
creases and flatten.

14

Lift up and repeat steps
10–13 on the right.

15

Lift up.

16

The model is 3D. Fold
along the creases.

17

Squash folds.

18

Fold and unfold.

19

Reverse folds.

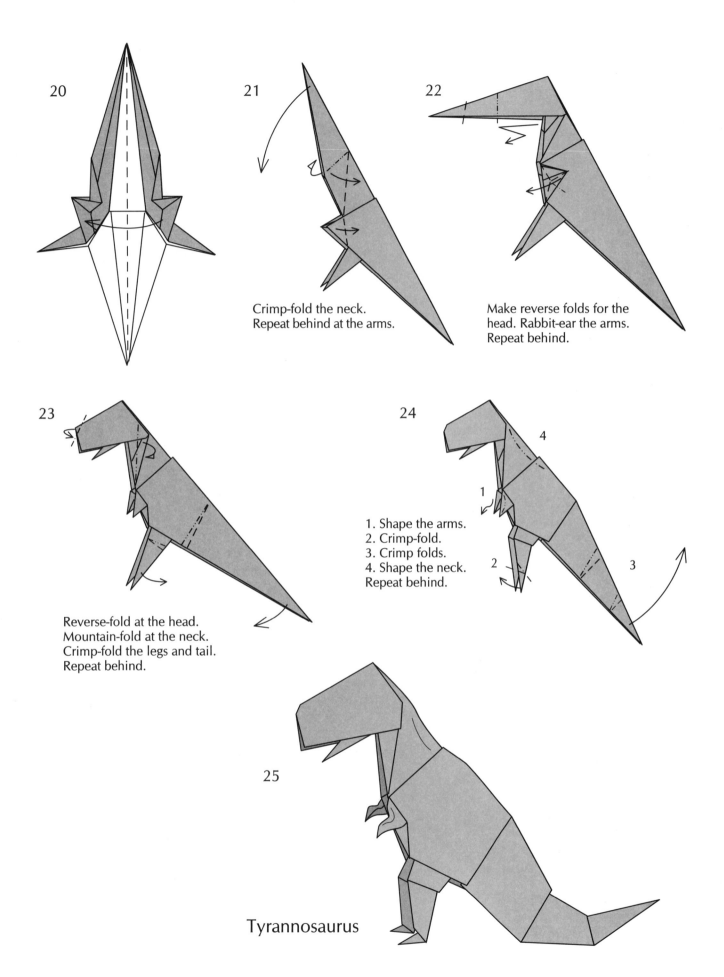

**20**

**21**

Crimp-fold the neck.
Repeat behind at the arms.

**22**

Make reverse folds for the
head. Rabbit-ear the arms.
Repeat behind.

**23**

Reverse-fold at the head.
Mountain-fold at the neck.
Crimp-fold the legs and tail.
Repeat behind.

**24**

4

1

1. Shape the arms.
2. Crimp-fold.
3. Crimp folds.
4. Shape the neck.
Repeat behind.

2

3

**25**

Tyrannosaurus

# Allosaurus

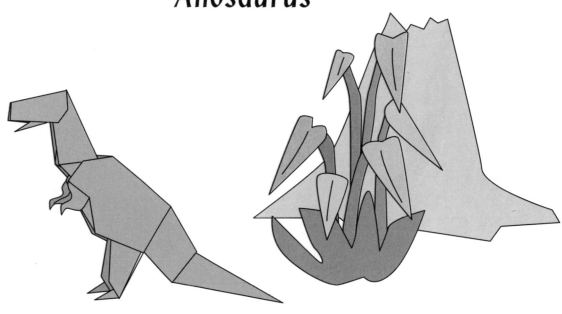

AL-us-saw-rus

This was the main meat eating dinosaur of the Jurassic period. It was 35 feet long. With a massive head and strong neck, it was able to unhinge its jaws like a snake does today and swallow huge hunks of meat. Also known as Antrodemus, fossils were found in Africa, Asia, and North America.

1

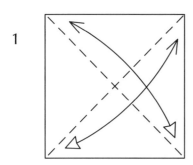

Fold and unfold.

2

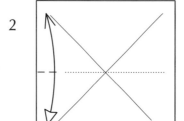

Fold and unfold on the left.

3

Bring the lower right corner to the top edge and the bottom edge to the left center. Crease on the right.

4

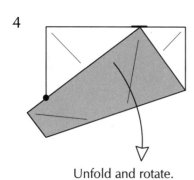

Unfold and rotate.

5

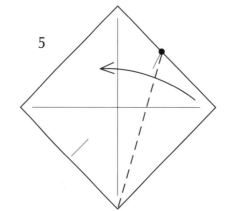

6

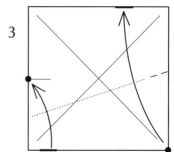

Squash-fold.

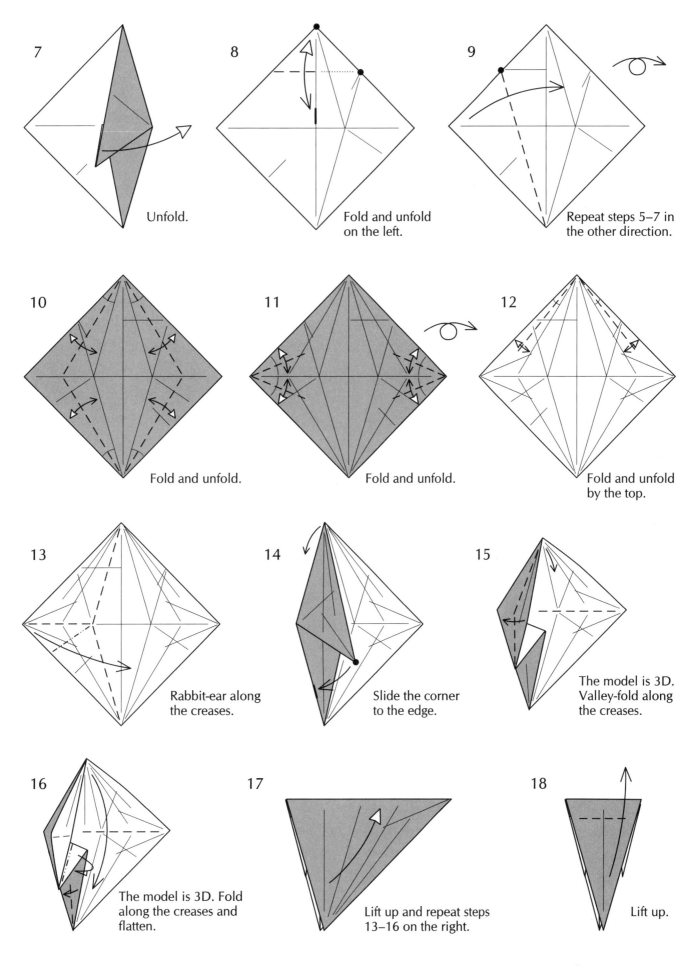

7 Unfold.

8 Fold and unfold on the left.

9 Repeat steps 5–7 in the other direction.

10 Fold and unfold.

11 Fold and unfold.

12 Fold and unfold by the top.

13 Rabbit-ear along the creases.

14 Slide the corner to the edge.

15 The model is 3D. Valley-fold along the creases.

16 The model is 3D. Fold along the creases and flatten.

17 Lift up and repeat steps 13–16 on the right.

18 Lift up.

*Allosaurus* 63

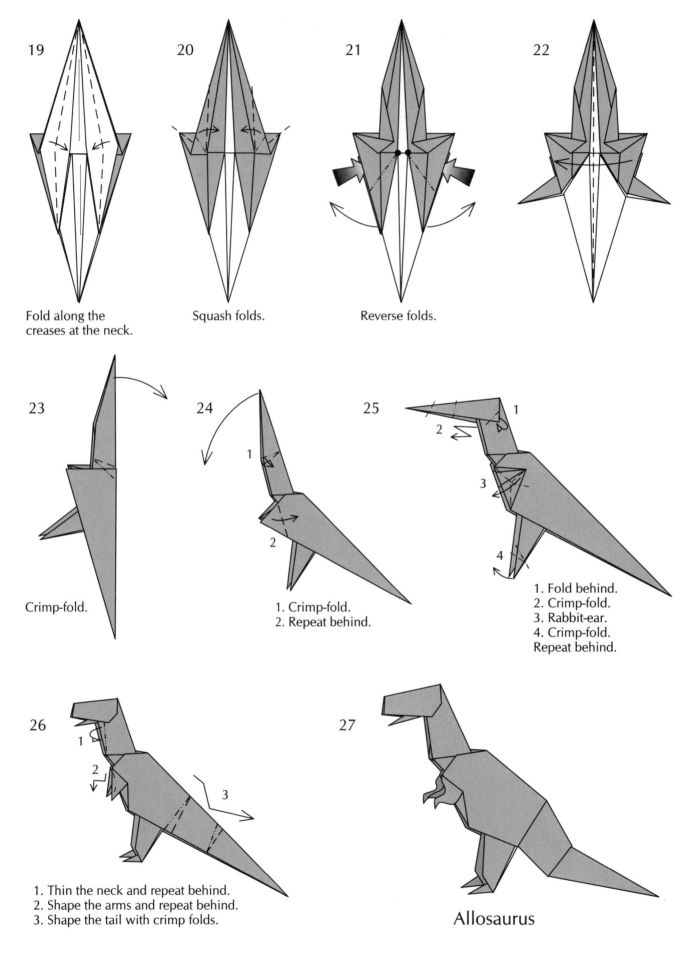

19

Fold along the
creases at the neck.

20

Squash folds.

21

Reverse folds.

22

23

Crimp-fold.

24

1. Crimp-fold.
2. Repeat behind.

25

1. Fold behind.
2. Crimp-fold.
3. Rabbit-ear.
4. Crimp-fold.
Repeat behind.

26

1. Thin the neck and repeat behind.
2. Shape the arms and repeat behind.
3. Shape the tail with crimp folds.

27

Allosaurus

# Parasaurolophus

par-a-SAUR-oh-loaf-us

A swamp dwelling, Cretaceous plant eater, this dinosaur was 33 feet long. The webbed feet and bill were not the only similarities to ducks. The long tubular crest on the top of the head may have enabled it to honk like a goose. It had grinding teeth in the back of the mouth. Parasaurolophus means "almost crest head" and it may have been the female to Corythosaurus.

Begin with step 20 of Allosaurus (page 62).

1

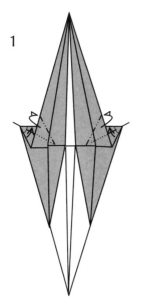

2

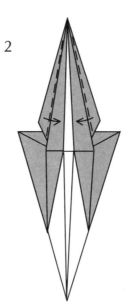

3

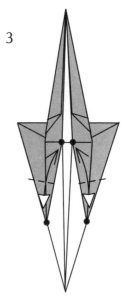

Fold and unfold.

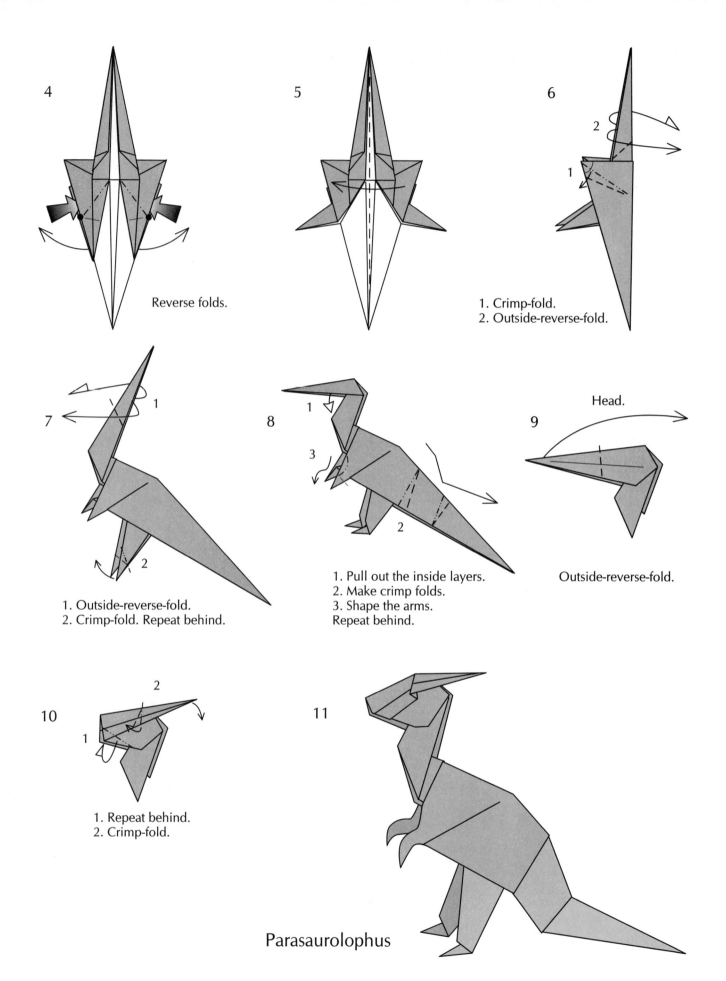

**4**

Reverse folds.

**5**

**6**

1. Crimp-fold.
2. Outside-reverse-fold.

**7**

1. Outside-reverse-fold.
2. Crimp-fold. Repeat behind.

**8**

1. Pull out the inside layers.
2. Make crimp folds.
3. Shape the arms.
Repeat behind.

**9**

Head.

Outside-reverse-fold.

**10**

1. Repeat behind.
2. Crimp-fold.

**11**

Parasaurolophus

# Coelophysis

see-low-FY-sis

This dinosaur has many characteristics of birds today. It had feathers, is believed to have been warm blooded, and had hollow bones, hence its name means "hollow form". It probably lived in family groups. It was 10 feet long and weighed 100 pounds. Fossils have been found in New Mexico and the eastern United States.

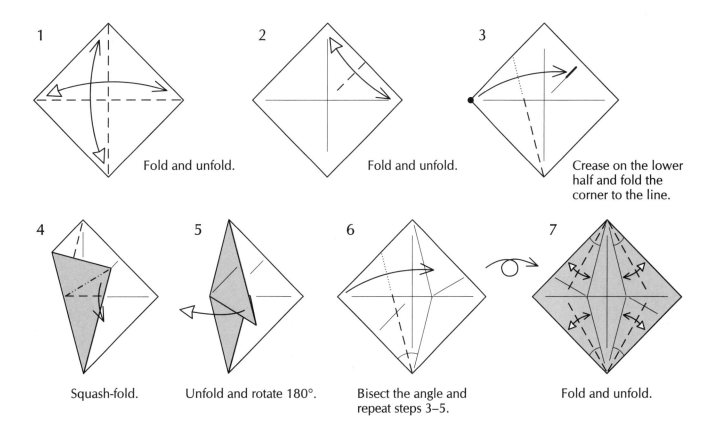

1

Fold and unfold.

2

Fold and unfold.

3

Crease on the lower half and fold the corner to the line.

4

Squash-fold.

5

Unfold and rotate 180°.

6

Bisect the angle and repeat steps 3–5.

7

Fold and unfold.

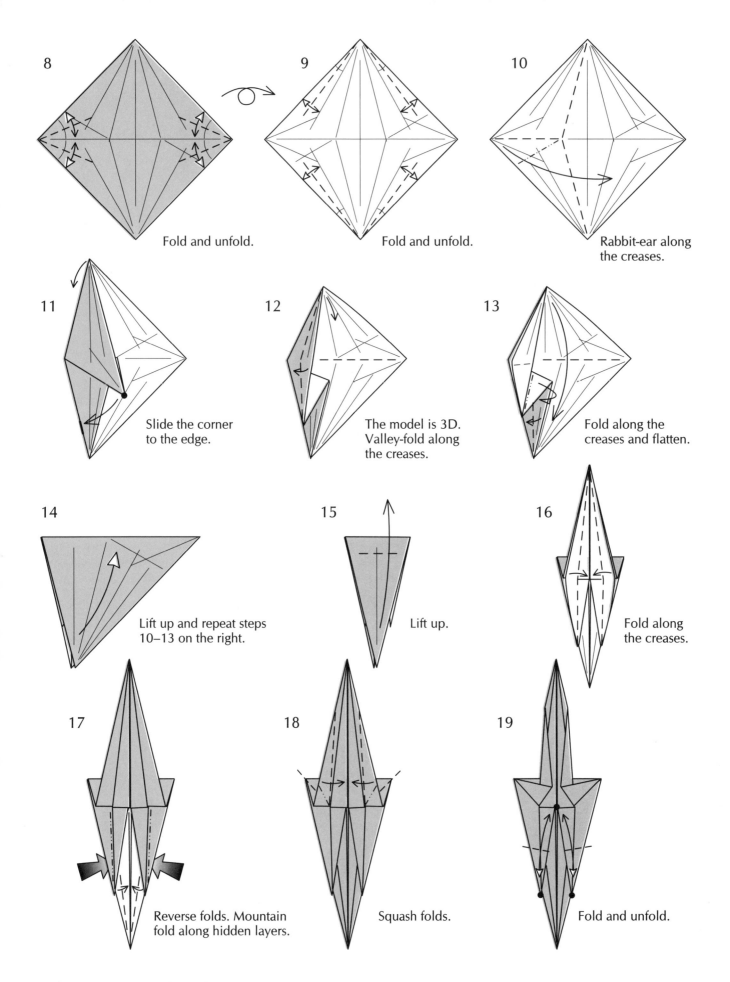

8 Fold and unfold.

9 Fold and unfold.

10 Rabbit-ear along the creases.

11 Slide the corner to the edge.

12 The model is 3D. Valley-fold along the creases.

13 Fold along the creases and flatten.

14 Lift up and repeat steps 10–13 on the right.

15 Lift up.

16 Fold along the creases.

17 Reverse folds. Mountain fold along hidden layers.

18 Squash folds.

19 Fold and unfold.

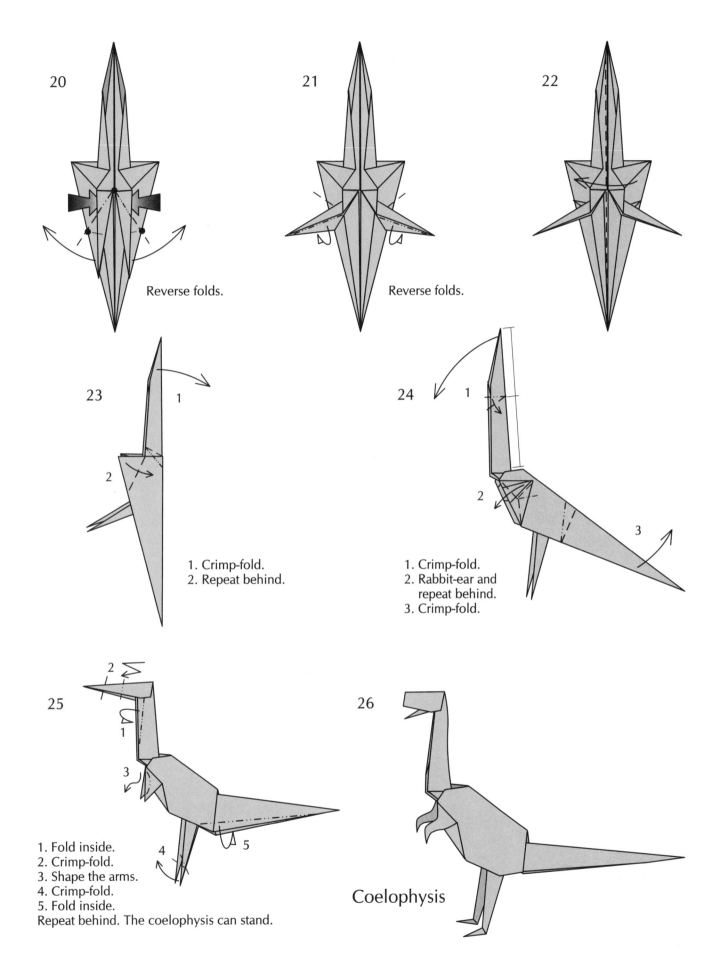

20

Reverse folds.

21

Reverse folds.

22

23

1
2

1. Crimp-fold.
2. Repeat behind.

24

1
2
3

1. Crimp-fold.
2. Rabbit-ear and
   repeat behind.
3. Crimp-fold.

25

2
1
3
4
5

1. Fold inside.
2. Crimp-fold.
3. Shape the arms.
4. Crimp-fold.
5. Fold inside.
Repeat behind. The coelophysis can stand.

26

Coelophysis

# Compsognathus

komp-so-NAY-thus

This tiny dinosaur was the size of a chicken and is one of the smallest dinosaurs ever found. It had hollow bones and bird-like legs. It ran swiftly around Jurassic Germany catching small reptiles and insects with its sharp claws. Its name means "elegant jaw".

1

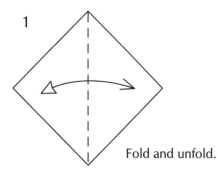

Fold and unfold.

2

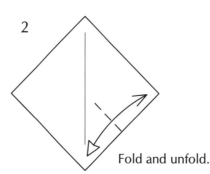

Fold and unfold.

3

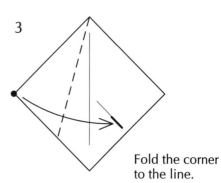

Fold the corner to the line.

4

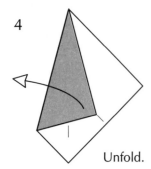

Unfold.

5

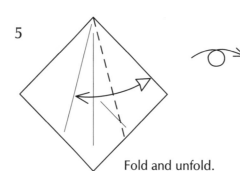

Fold and unfold.

6

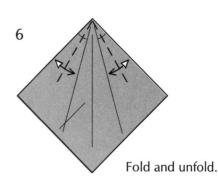

Fold and unfold.

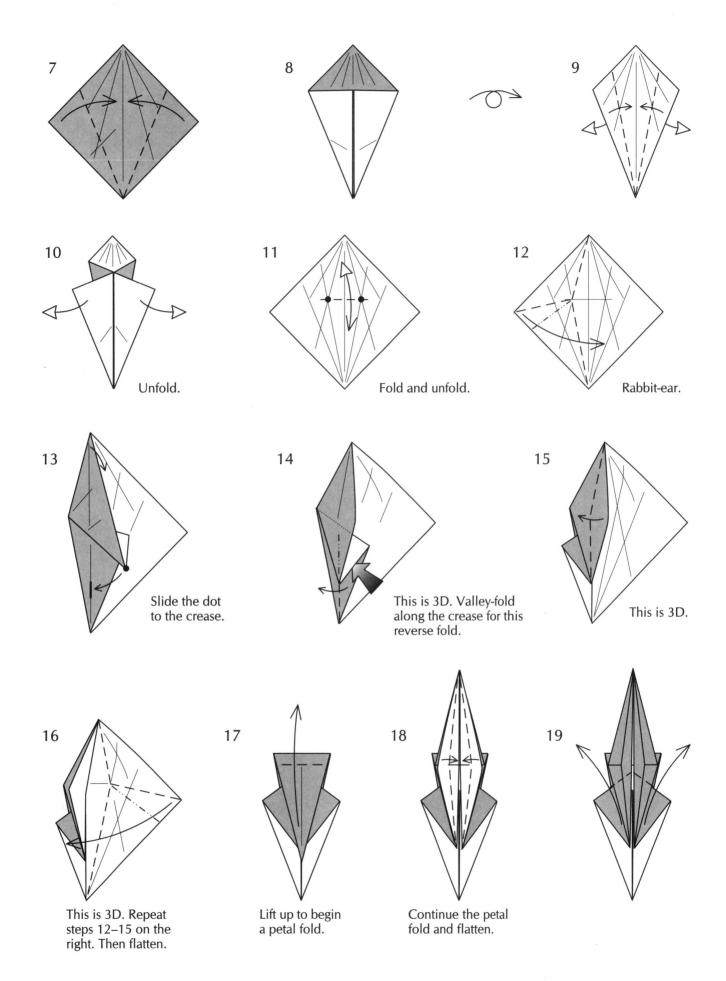

7

8

9

10

Unfold.

11

Fold and unfold.

12

Rabbit-ear.

13

Slide the dot
to the crease.

14

This is 3D. Valley-fold
along the crease for this
reverse fold.

15

This is 3D.

16

This is 3D. Repeat
steps 12–15 on the
right. Then flatten.

17

Lift up to begin
a petal fold.

18

Continue the petal
fold and flatten.

19

*Compsognathus* 71

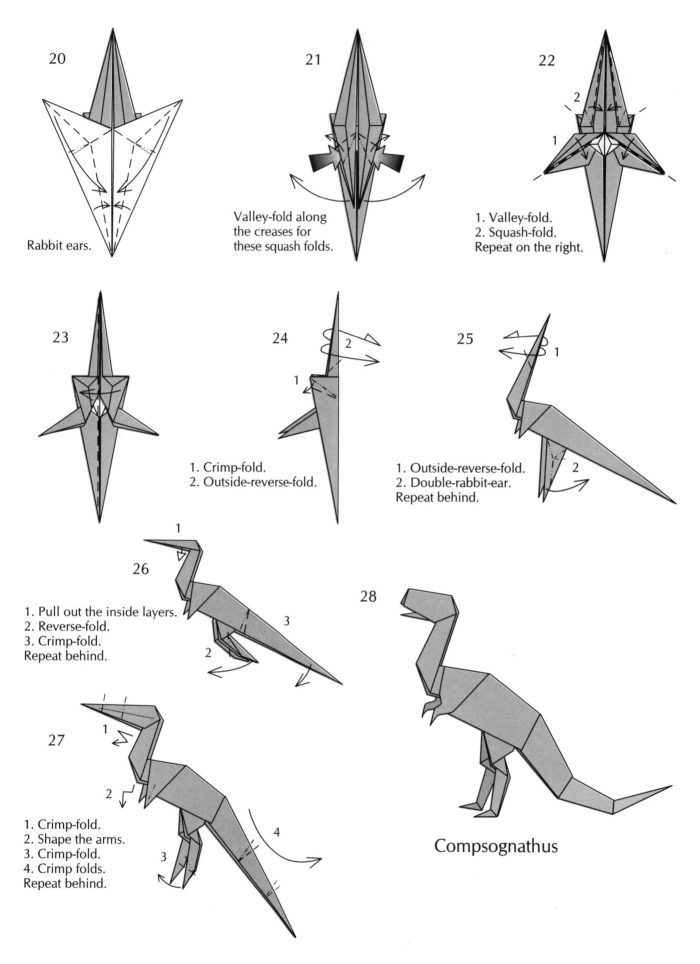

20

Rabbit ears.

21

Valley-fold along
the creases for
these squash folds.

22

1. Valley-fold.
2. Squash-fold.
Repeat on the right.

23

24

1. Crimp-fold.
2. Outside-reverse-fold.

25

1. Outside-reverse-fold.
2. Double-rabbit-ear.
Repeat behind.

26

1. Pull out the inside layers.
2. Reverse-fold.
3. Crimp-fold.
Repeat behind.

27

1. Crimp-fold.
2. Shape the arms.
3. Crimp-fold.
4. Crimp folds.
Repeat behind.

28

Compsognathus

# Sphaerotholus

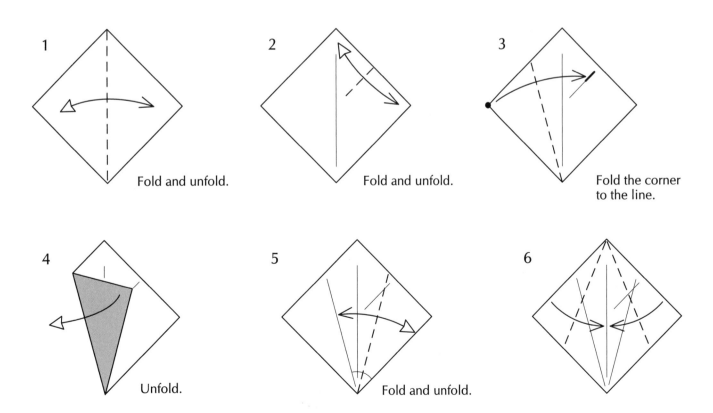

SPHERE-oh-THOLE-us

This dinosaur belongs to the pachycephalosaur family of bone-headed dinosaur known for their thick skull bones. Sphaerotholus means "ball-dome". They traveled in herds and may have butted their heads together to compete for territory. It is a plant eater and lived in the Cretaceous Period. Fossils have been found in the western US.

1

Fold and unfold.

2

Fold and unfold.

3

Fold the corner to the line.

4

Unfold.

5

Fold and unfold.

6

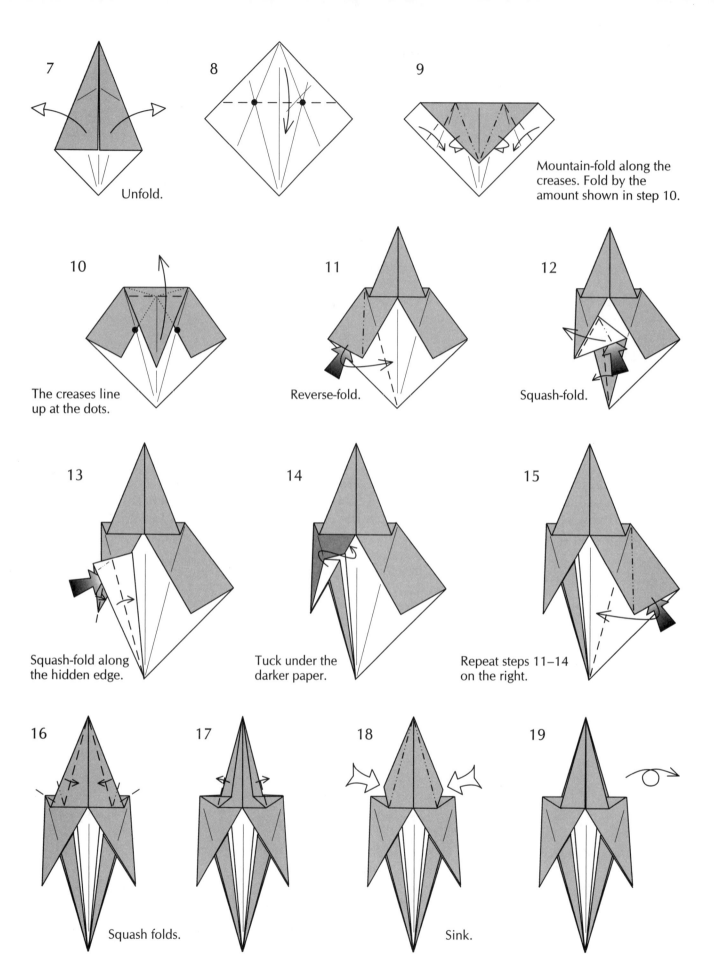

**7**

Unfold.

**8**

**9**

Mountain-fold along the creases. Fold by the amount shown in step 10.

**10**

The creases line up at the dots.

**11**

Reverse-fold.

**12**

Squash-fold.

**13**

Squash-fold along the hidden edge.

**14**

Tuck under the darker paper.

**15**

Repeat steps 11–14 on the right.

**16**

Squash folds.

**17**

**18**

Sink.

**19**

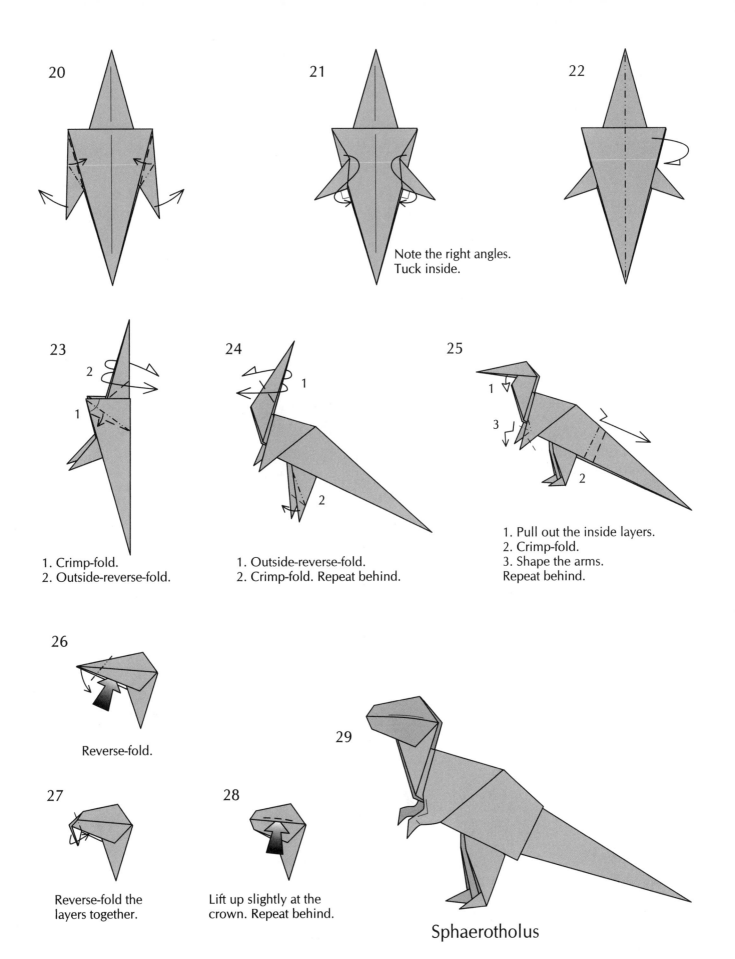

20

21

Note the right angles.
Tuck inside.

22

23

1. Crimp-fold.
2. Outside-reverse-fold.

24

1. Outside-reverse-fold.
2. Crimp-fold. Repeat behind.

25

1. Pull out the inside layers.
2. Crimp-fold.
3. Shape the arms.
Repeat behind.

26

Reverse-fold.

27

Reverse-fold the
layers together.

28

Lift up slightly at the
crown. Repeat behind.

29

Sphaerotholus

# Struthiomimus

strooth-ee-oh-MIM-us

This 12 foot long Cretaceous dinosaur was probably as swift as an ostrich. The name means "ostrich mimic". It had no teeth in its beak and used its three-fingered hands to dig and grasp food. The tail helped it balance. Fossils were found in New Jersey and Canada.

Begin with step 21 of Sphaerotholus (page 73).

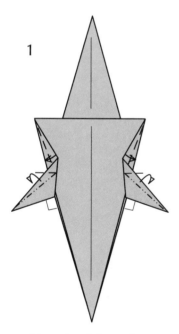

1

Note the right angles.

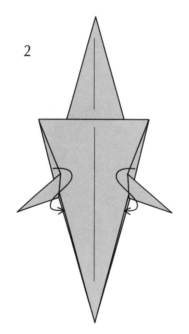

2

Tuck inside.

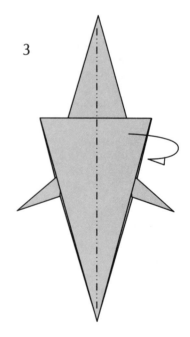

3

4

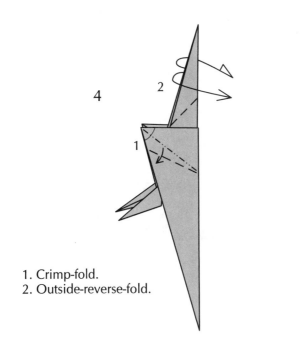

1. Crimp-fold.
2. Outside-reverse-fold.

5

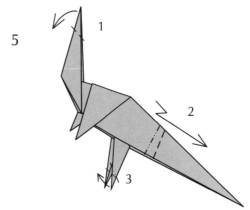

1. Outside-reverse-fold.
2. Crimp-fold.
3. Crimp-fold. Repeat behind.

6

1. Pull out the inside layers.
2. Reverse-fold.
3. Shape the arms.
4. Shape the back and tail.
5. Shape the legs.
Repeat behind.

7

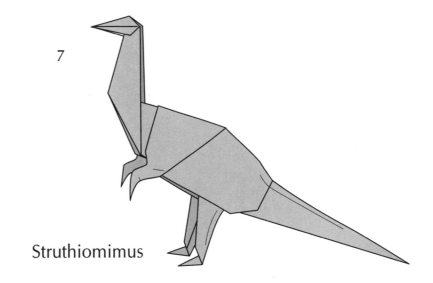

Struthiomimus

# Tenontosaurus

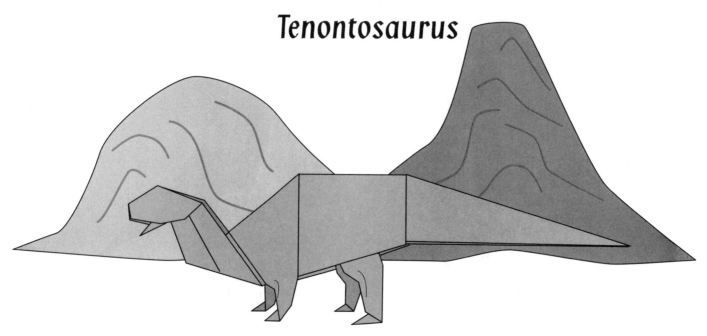

ten-ON-tuh-sawr-us

This 20 foot long Cretaceous plant eater resembled Iguanodon but did not have spiked thumbs. His name means "tendon lizard" because it had rod-like tendons, tendons that held its tail rigid when it ran. Fossils have been found in Montana, Wyoming, Texas, and Oklahoma.

Begin with step 17 of Sphaerotholus (page 73).

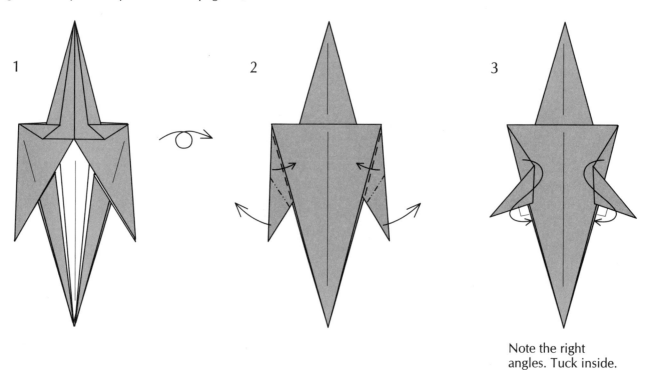

1

2

3

Note the right angles. Tuck inside.

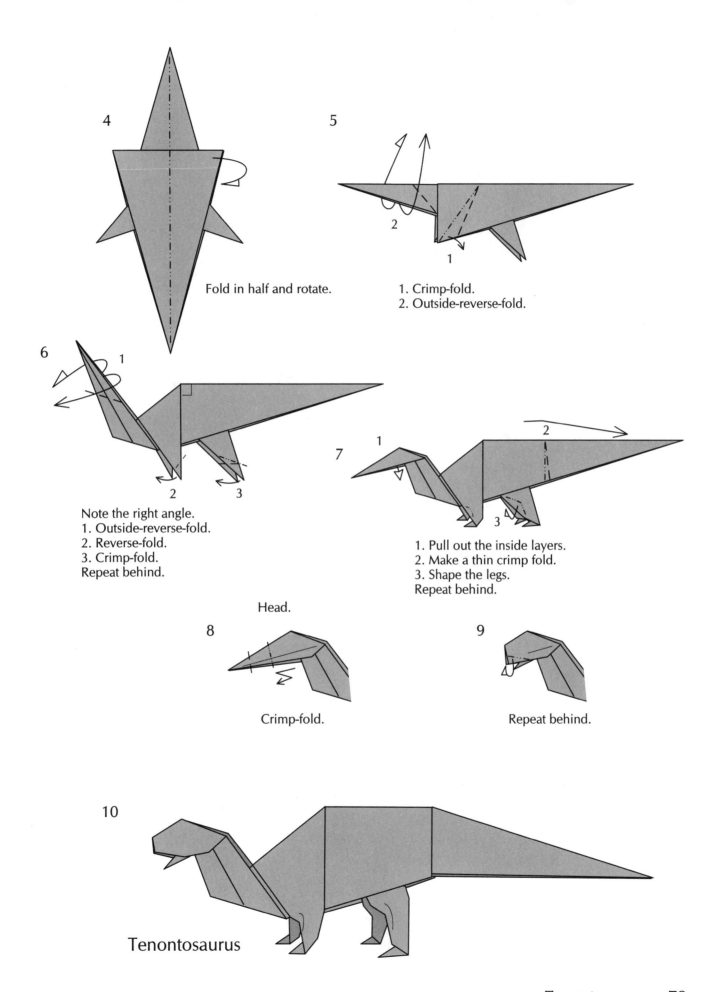

4

Fold in half and rotate.

5

1. Crimp-fold.
2. Outside-reverse-fold.

6

Note the right angle.
1. Outside-reverse-fold.
2. Reverse-fold.
3. Crimp-fold.
Repeat behind.

7

1. Pull out the inside layers.
2. Make a thin crimp fold.
3. Shape the legs.
Repeat behind.

Head.

8

Crimp-fold.

9

Repeat behind.

10

Tenontosaurus

# Apatosaurus

a-PAT-oh-saw-rus

This dinosaur is better known as Brontosaurus, the "thunder lizard" but more correctly named Apatosaurus, the "headless lizard". It was 70 feet long and very heavy. The front legs were shorter than the back legs. Its fossils were found in the western U.S. with other Jurassic dinosaurs. Its small flat teeth could not have ground up all the food required to fuel this animal so it relied on "gizzard stones" to aid in digestion.

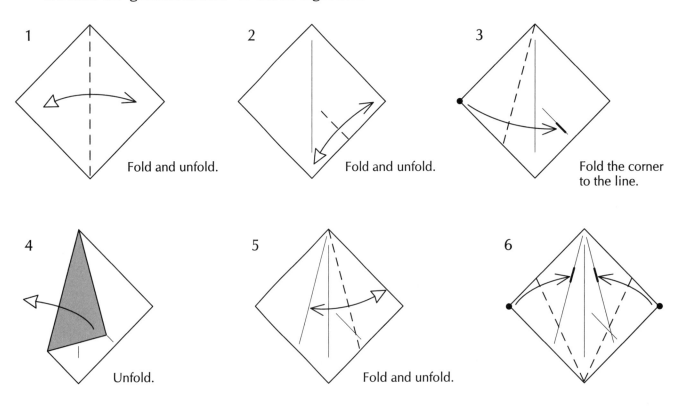

1 Fold and unfold.

2 Fold and unfold.

3 Fold the corner to the line.

4 Unfold.

5 Fold and unfold.

6

4

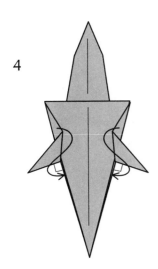

Note the right angles.
Tuck inside.

5

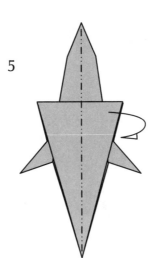

6

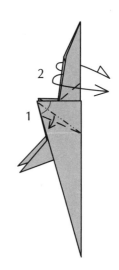

1. Crimp-fold.
2. Outside-reverse-fold.

7

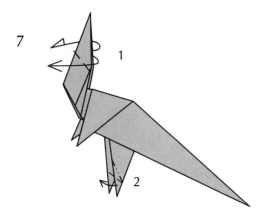

1. Outside-reverse-fold.
2. Crimp-fold. Repeat behind.

8

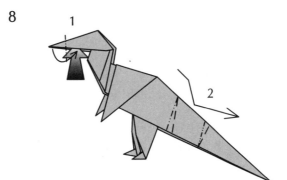

1. Reverse-fold.
2. Make crimp folds.

9

1. Crimp-fold.
2. Shape the arms. Repeat behind.

10

Gryposaurus

# Hadrosaurus

had-ro-SAW-rus

Formerly known as Trachodon, the "rough tooth", this duck billed dinosaur was 33 feet long. Behind the bill were 2000 teeth used for grinding water plants. Hadrosaurus means "bulky lizard" and it was the first dinosaur skeleton ever excavated in the U.S. It was found in New Jersey in 1858. Mummified skin of this Cretaceous creature has also been found.

1

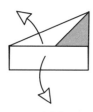

Fold and unfold.

2

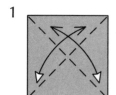

Fold and unfold.

3

4

5

Unfold.

6

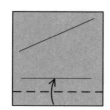

7

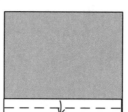

8

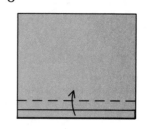

Fold along the existing crease.

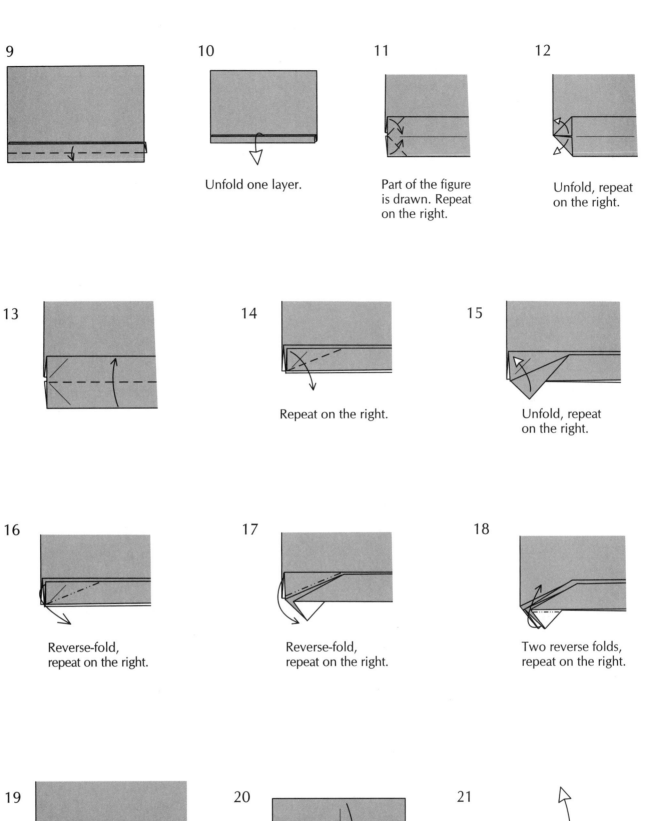

9

10

Unfold one layer.

11

Part of the figure
is drawn. Repeat
on the right.

12

Unfold, repeat
on the right.

13

14

Repeat on the right.

15

Unfold, repeat
on the right.

16

Reverse-fold,
repeat on the right.

17

Reverse-fold,
repeat on the right.

18

Two reverse folds,
repeat on the right.

19

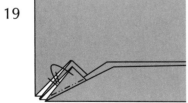

Two reverse folds,
repeat on the right.

20

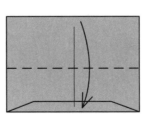

21

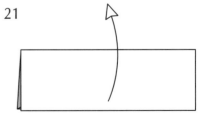

Unfold.

**22**

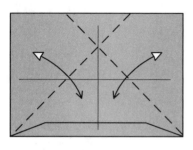

Fold and unfold.

**23**

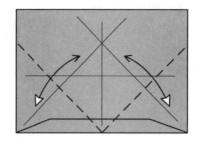

Fold and unfold.

**24**

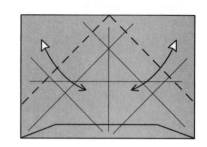

Fold and unfold.

**25**

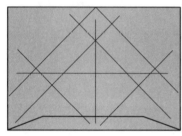

**26**

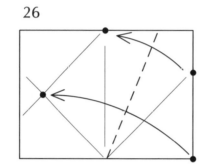

The dots will meet.

**27**

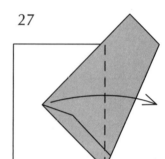

**28**

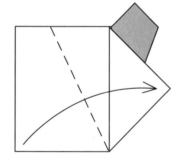

**29**

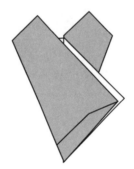

**30**

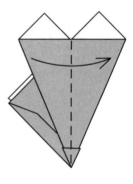

**31**

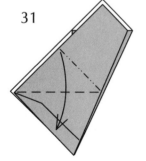

Squash-fold.

**32**

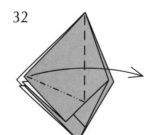

Repeat behind.

**33**

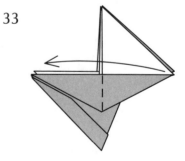

Repeat behind.

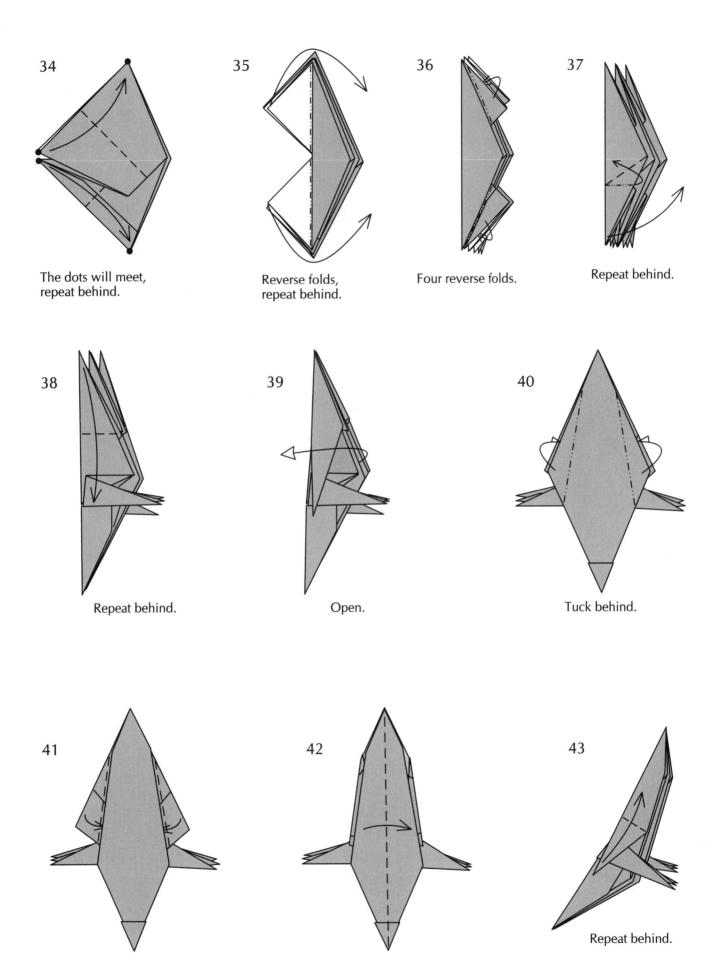

34 The dots will meet, repeat behind.

35 Reverse folds, repeat behind.

36 Four reverse folds.

37 Repeat behind.

38 Repeat behind.

39 Open.

40 Tuck behind.

41

42

43 Repeat behind.

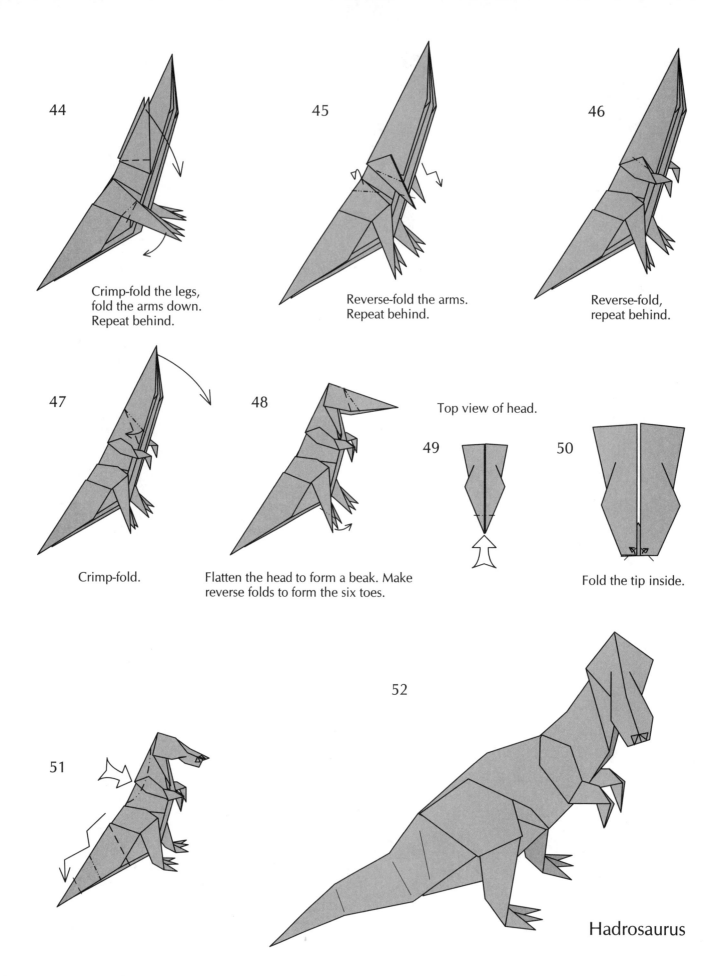

**44**

Crimp-fold the legs,
fold the arms down.
Repeat behind.

**45**

Reverse-fold the arms.
Repeat behind.

**46**

Reverse-fold,
repeat behind.

**47**

Crimp-fold.

**48**

Flatten the head to form a beak. Make
reverse folds to form the six toes.

Top view of head.

**49**

**50**

Fold the tip inside.

**51**

**52**

Hadrosaurus

# Iguanodon

i-GWA-no-don

The most distinguishing feature of this Cretaceous dinosaur is the spike-like thumbs on its front legs. Standing on its hind legs, this reptile stood 16 feet tall. However, it could also have walked on four legs. It had grinding teeth in the back of its mouth and a strong beak to break off plants. One of the first dinosaurs ever discovered, fossils were found in Belgium and North Africa. Iguanodon means "iguana tooth".

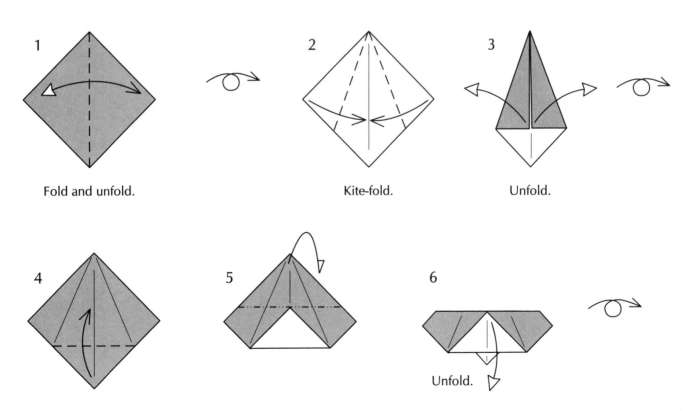

1
Fold and unfold.

2
Kite-fold.

3
Unfold.

4

5

6
Unfold.

7

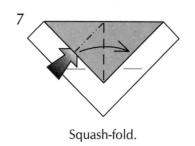

Squash-fold.

8

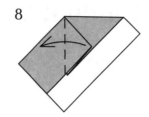

9

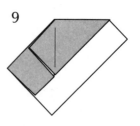

Repeat steps 7–8
on the right.

10

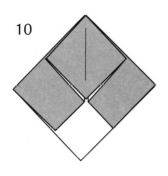

11

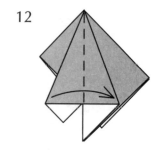

Squash-fold.

12

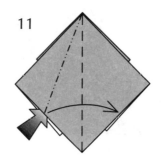

13

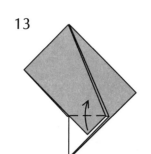

14

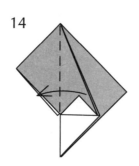

15

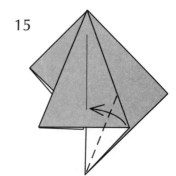

16

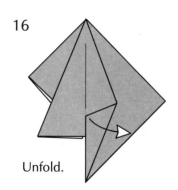

Unfold.

17

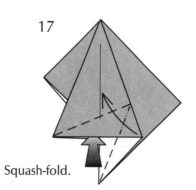

Squash-fold.

18

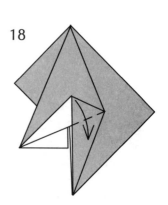

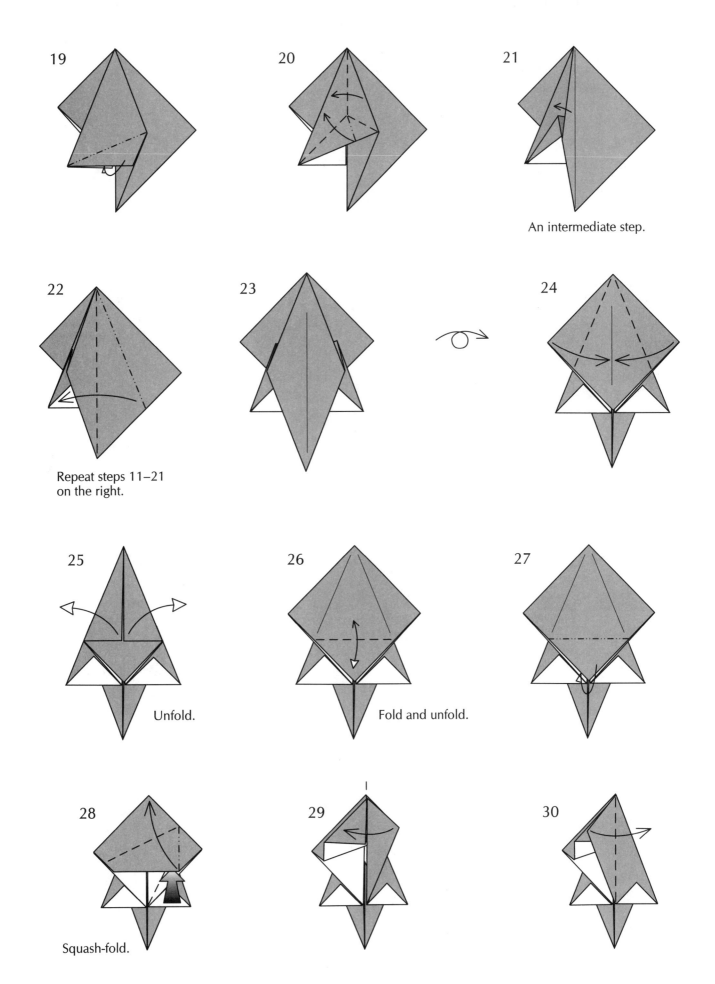

19

20

21

An intermediate step.

22

Repeat steps 11–21
on the right.

23

24

25

Unfold.

26

Fold and unfold.

27

28

Squash-fold.

29

30

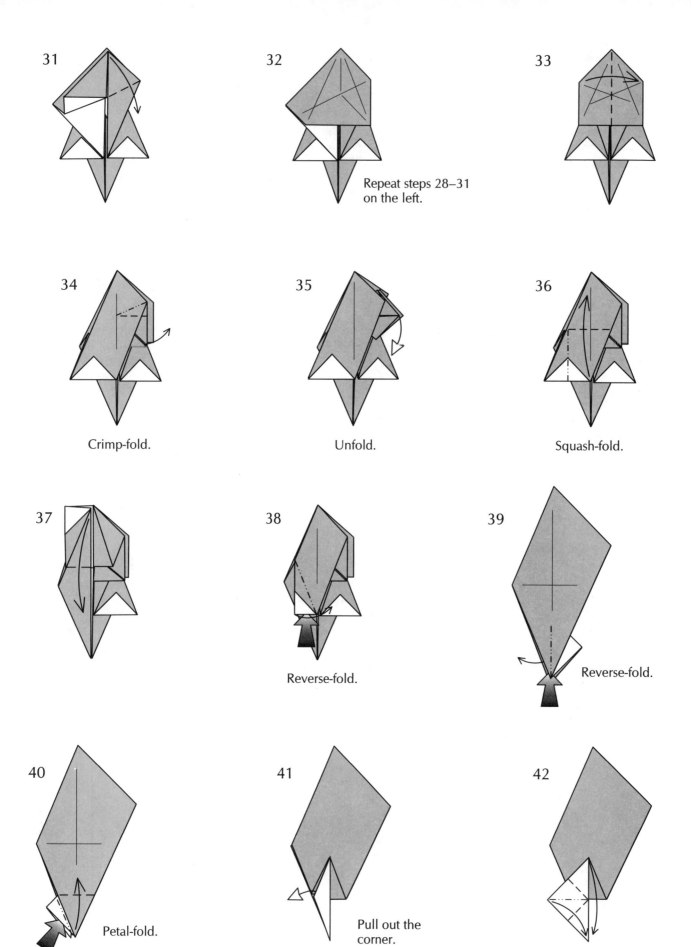

31

32

Repeat steps 28–31
on the left.

33

34

Crimp-fold.

35

Unfold.

36

Squash-fold.

37

38

Reverse-fold.

39

Reverse-fold.

40

Petal-fold.

41

Pull out the
corner.

42

43

Reverse folds.

44

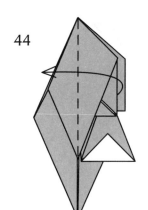

45

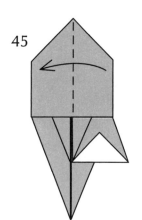

46

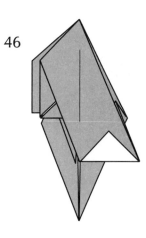

Repeat steps 36–44
on the right.

47

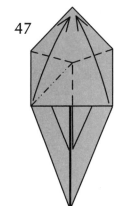

Bring the corners
to the top.

48

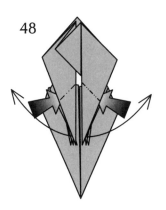

Reverse folds.

49

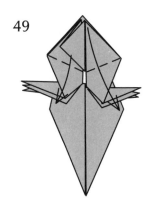

50

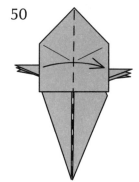

51

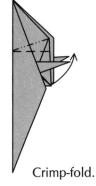

Crimp-fold.

52

Repeat behind.

53

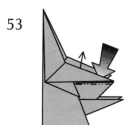

Reverse-fold.

54

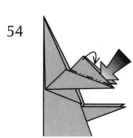

Reverse-fold.

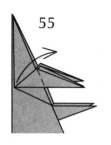

55

Repeat behind.

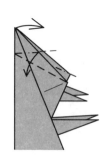

56

Crimp-fold.

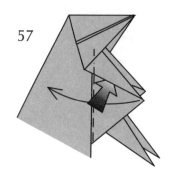

57

Reverse-fold,
repeat behind.

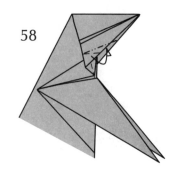

58

Repeat behind.

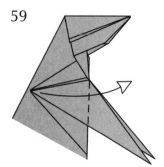

59

Unfold, repeat behind.

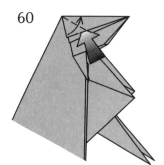

60

Unlock the top layer,
repeat behind.

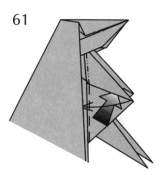

61

Reverse-fold, tuck under the
top layer. Repeat behind.

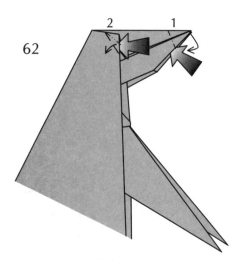

62

1. Reverse-fold the tip.
2. Squash-fold the eye,
   repeat behind.

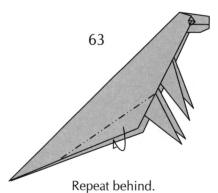

63

Repeat behind.

64

Legs.

Reverse-fold,
repeat behind.

**65**

Reverse folds,
repeat behind.

**66**

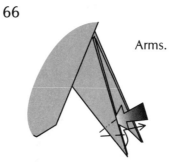

Arms.

Form the thumb with two
reverse folds, repeat behind.

**67**

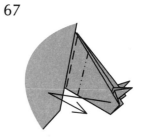

Repeat behind.

**68**

Shape the arms and
hands, repeat behind.

**69**

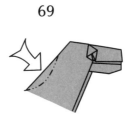

Shape the neck.

**70**

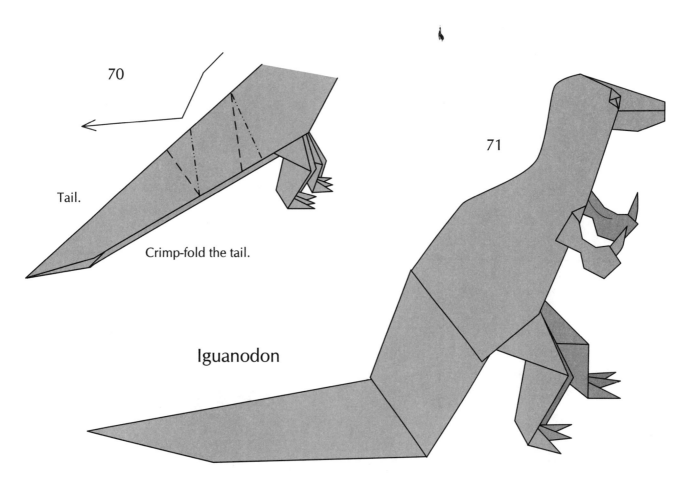

Tail.

Crimp-fold the tail.

Iguanodon

**71**

# Protoceratops

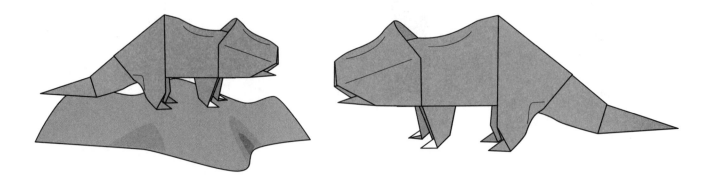

pro-toe-SER-a-tops

The "first horn face" fossils were discovered in Mongolia and showed paleontologists how dinosaurs may have cared for their young. The nests included unhatched eggs as well as skeletons of babies. The adults grew to 6 feet long. These were Cretaceous plant eaters with parrot-like beaks and bone covered faces.

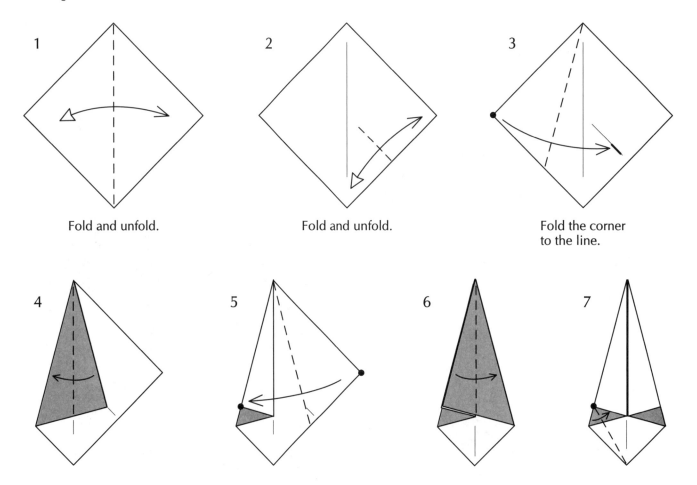

1

Fold and unfold.

2

Fold and unfold.

3

Fold the corner to the line.

4

5

6

7

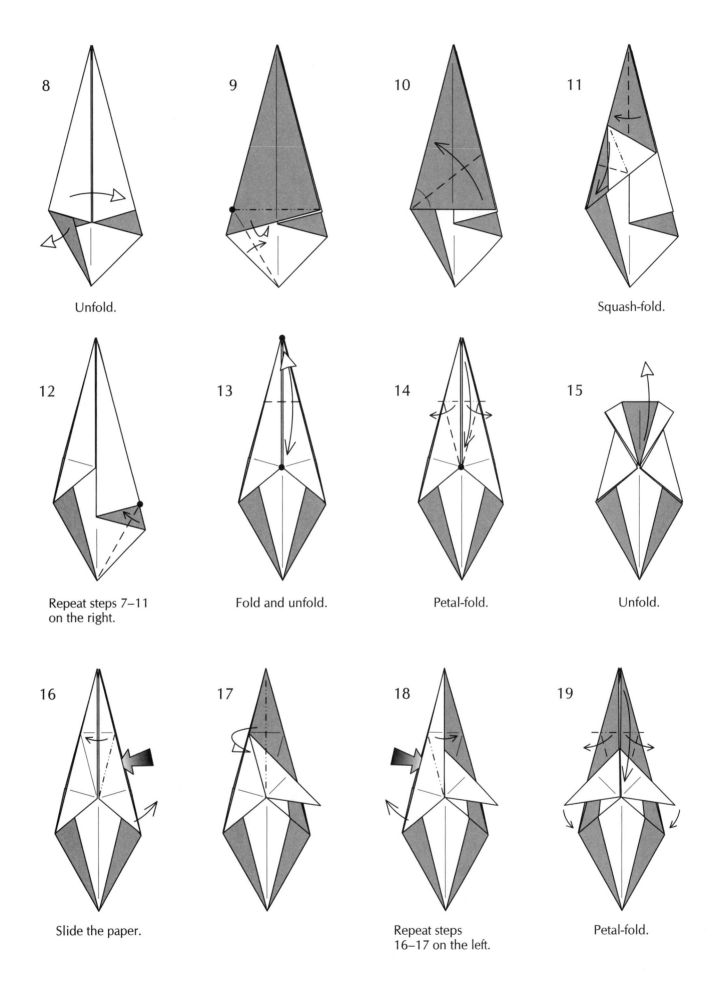

8 Unfold.

9

10

11 Squash-fold.

12 Repeat steps 7–11 on the right.

13 Fold and unfold.

14 Petal-fold.

15 Unfold.

16 Slide the paper.

17

18 Repeat steps 16–17 on the left.

19 Petal-fold.

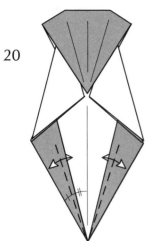

20

Fold and unfold at an
angle of about one-third.

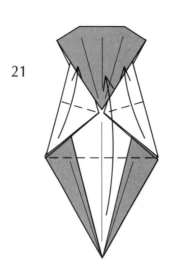

21

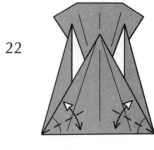

22

Fold and unfold.

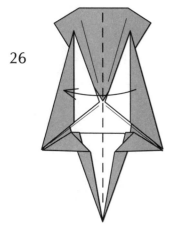

23

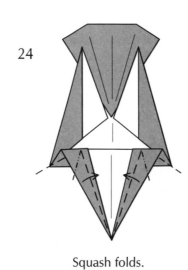

24

Squash folds.

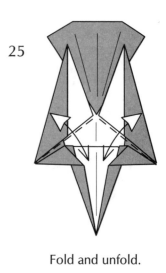

25

Fold and unfold.

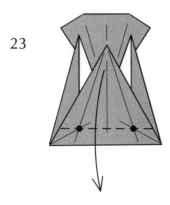

26

Fold in half and rotate.

27

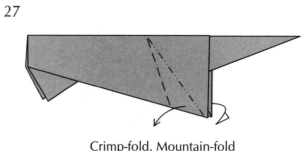

Crimp-fold. Mountain-fold
along the crease.

**28**

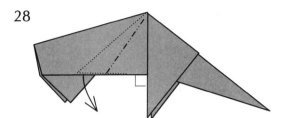

Note the right angle. Reverse-fold
the front leg. Repeat behind.

**29**

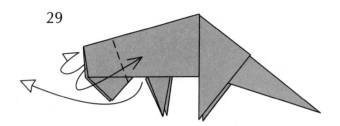

Outside-reverse-fold the head
and pull out the hidden corner.

**30**

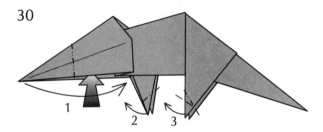

1. Reverse-fold.
2. Reverse-fold.
3. Crimp-fold.
Repeat behind.

**31**

1. Repeat behind.
2. Reverse-fold the mouth.
3. Crimp-fold the tail.

**32**

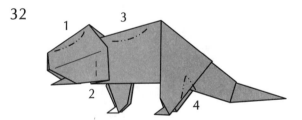

Shape the model.

**33**

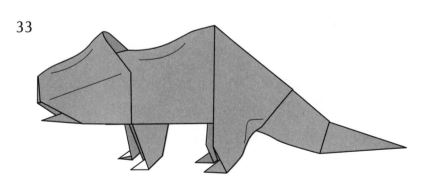

Protoceratops

# Styracosaurus

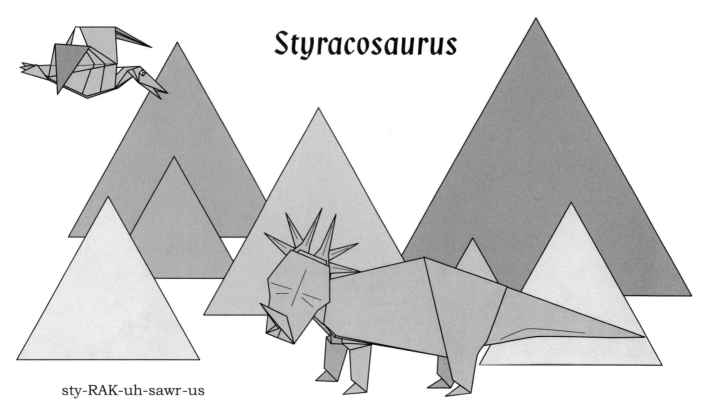

sty-RAK-uh-sawr-us

Even though this 18 foot long ceratopsian weighed 3 tons, scientist believe it was a good runner. It may have gone as fast as 20 miles an hour. It lived at the end of the Cretaceous Period and its fossils were found in Alberta, Canada. Styracosaurus means "spiked lizard".

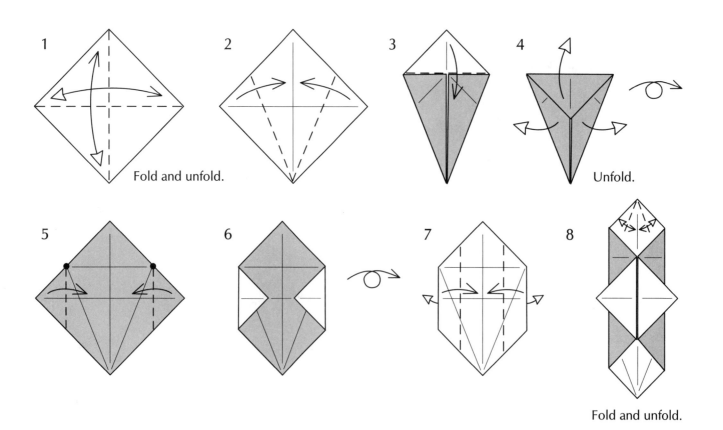

1
Fold and unfold.

2

3

4
Unfold.

5

6

7

8
Fold and unfold.

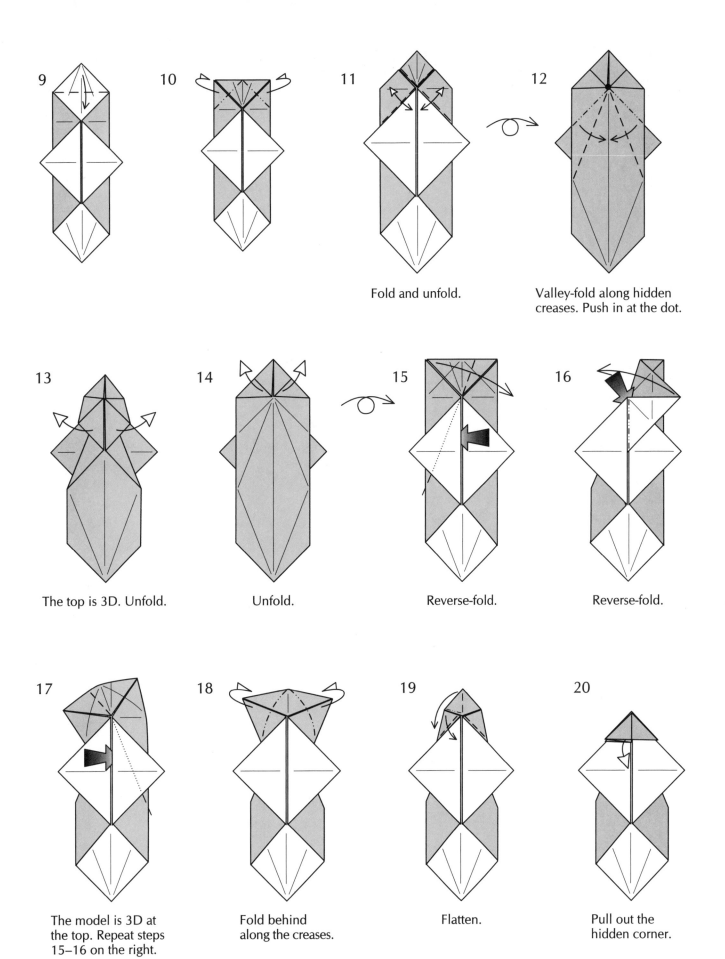

9

10

11

Fold and unfold.

12

Valley-fold along hidden creases. Push in at the dot.

13

The top is 3D. Unfold.

14

Unfold.

15

Reverse-fold.

16

Reverse-fold.

17

The model is 3D at the top. Repeat steps 15–16 on the right.

18

Fold behind along the creases.

19

Flatten.

20

Pull out the hidden corner.

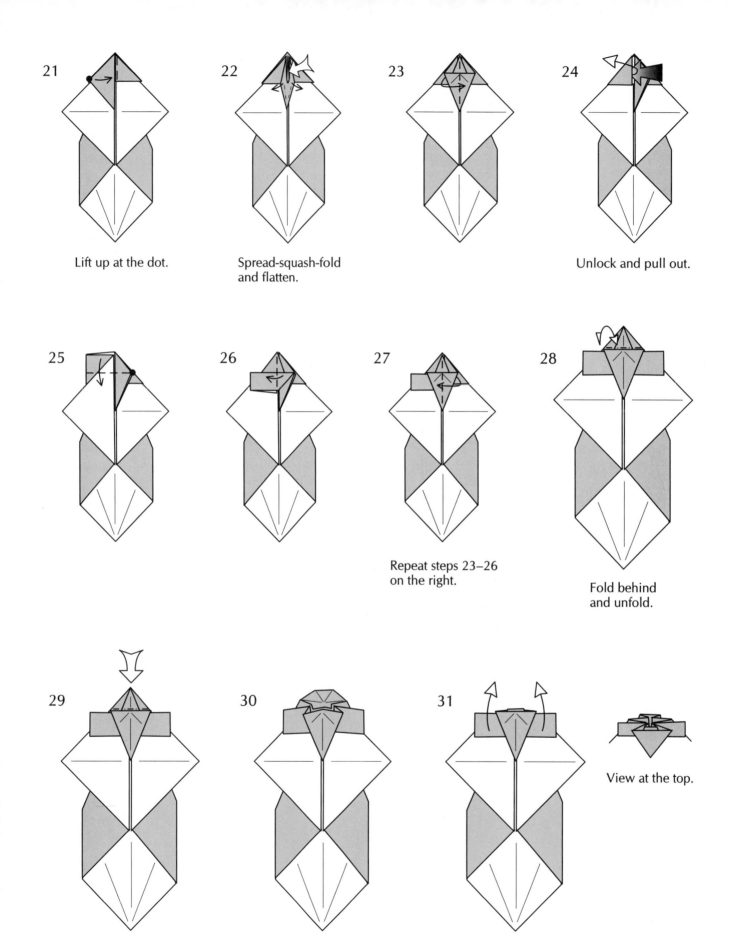

21 Lift up at the dot.

22 Spread-squash-fold and flatten.

23

24 Unlock and pull out.

25

26

27 Repeat steps 23–26 on the right.

28 Fold behind and unfold.

29 Sink.

30 Intermediate step.

31 Unfold.

View at the top.

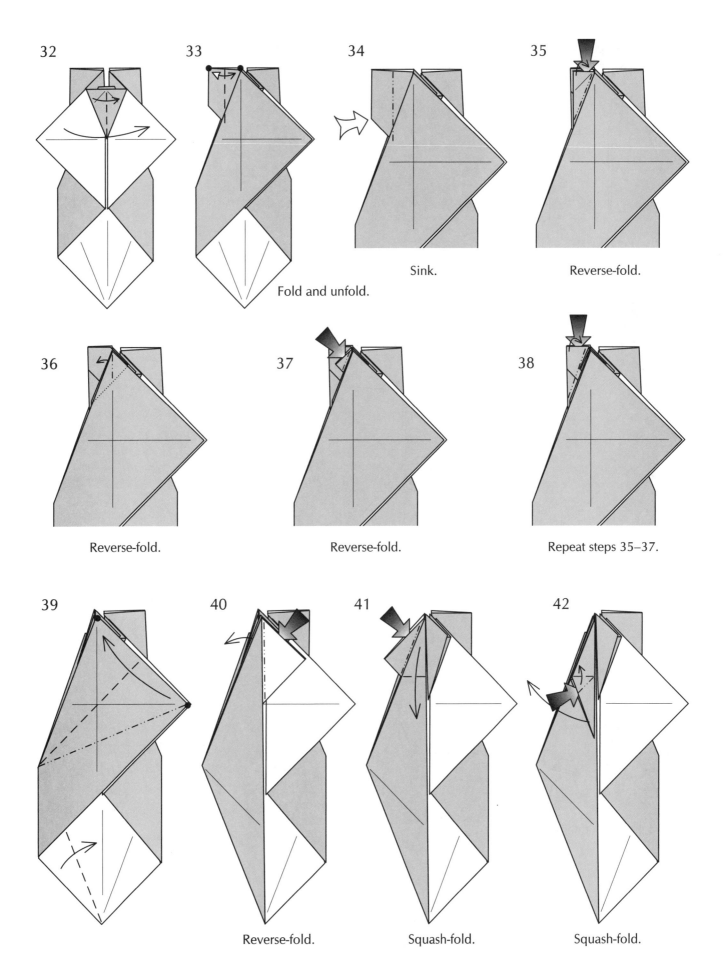

32

33

Fold and unfold.

34

Sink.

35

Reverse-fold.

36

Reverse-fold.

37

Reverse-fold.

38

Repeat steps 35–37.

39

40

Reverse-fold.

41

Squash-fold.

42

Squash-fold.

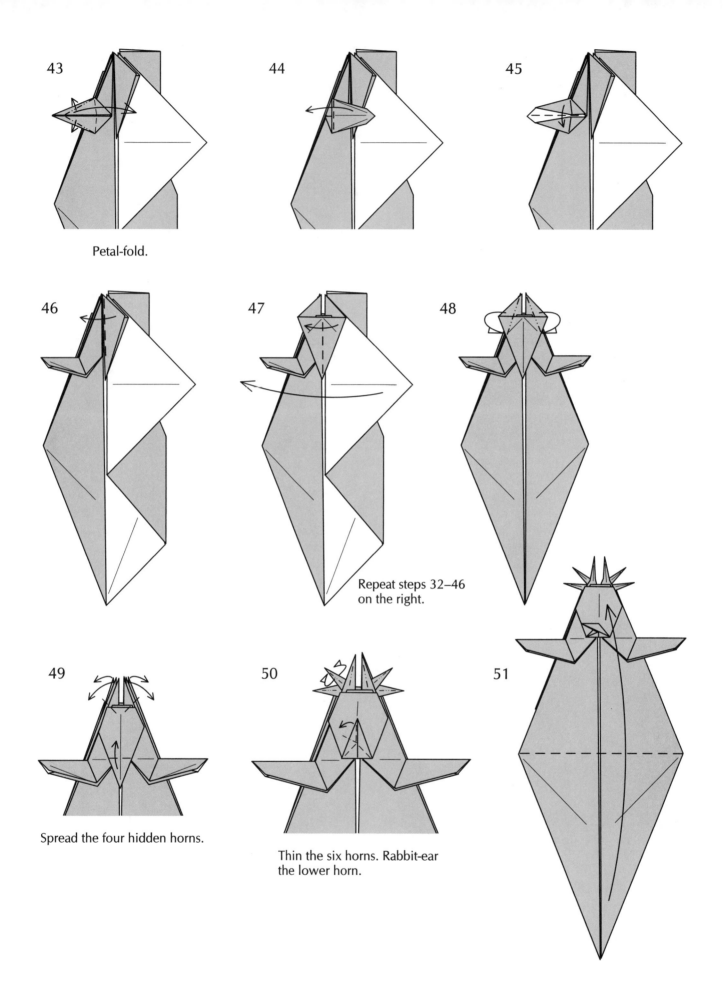

43

Petal-fold.

44

45

46

47

Repeat steps 32–46
on the right.

48

49

Spread the four hidden horns.

50

Thin the six horns. Rabbit-ear
the lower horn.

51

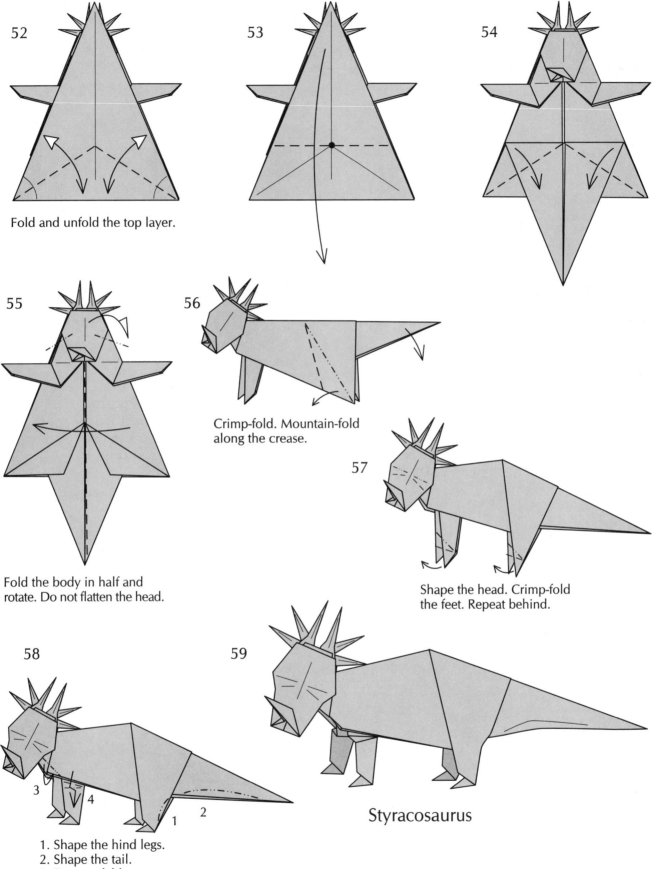

52

Fold and unfold the top layer.

53

54

55

Fold the body in half and rotate. Do not flatten the head.

56

Crimp-fold. Mountain-fold along the crease.

57

Shape the head. Crimp-fold the feet. Repeat behind.

58

1. Shape the hind legs.
2. Shape the tail.
3. Reverse-fold.
4. Shape the front legs.
Repeat behind.

59

Styracosaurus

# Triceratops

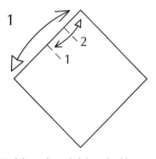

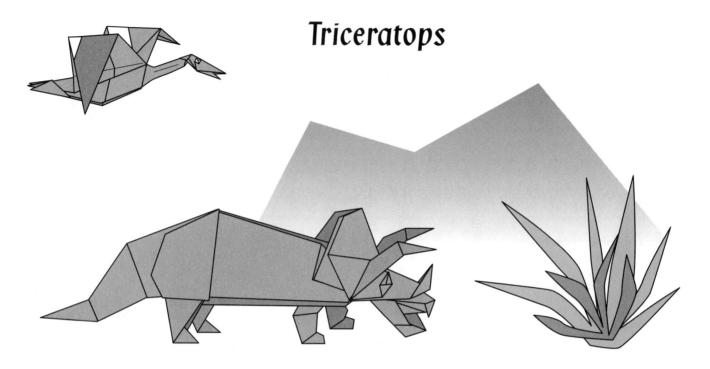

try-SER-a-tops

A peaceful plant eater, Triceratops was 30 feet long. It had a beak like a parrot. Its name means "three horn face" and the horns over its eyes were 3 feet long. The tough, leathery skin and the bony frill protecting its neck made Triceratops one of the best protected dinosaurs. It is thought to be the last one to succumb to extinction at the end of the Cretaceous.

**1**

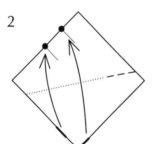

Fold and unfold in half twice. Only crease by the edge.

**2**

Bring the edges to the dots. Crease on the right.

**3**

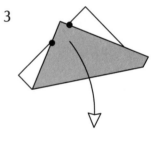

Unfold.

**4**

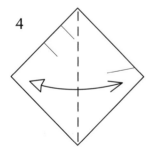

Fold and unfold.

**5**

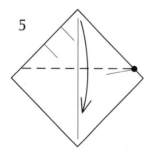

Robert Lang's ReferenceFinder software was used to find the landmark at the dot.

**6**

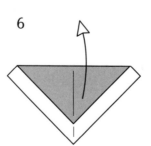

Unfold.

**7**

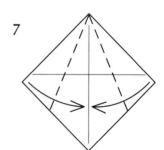

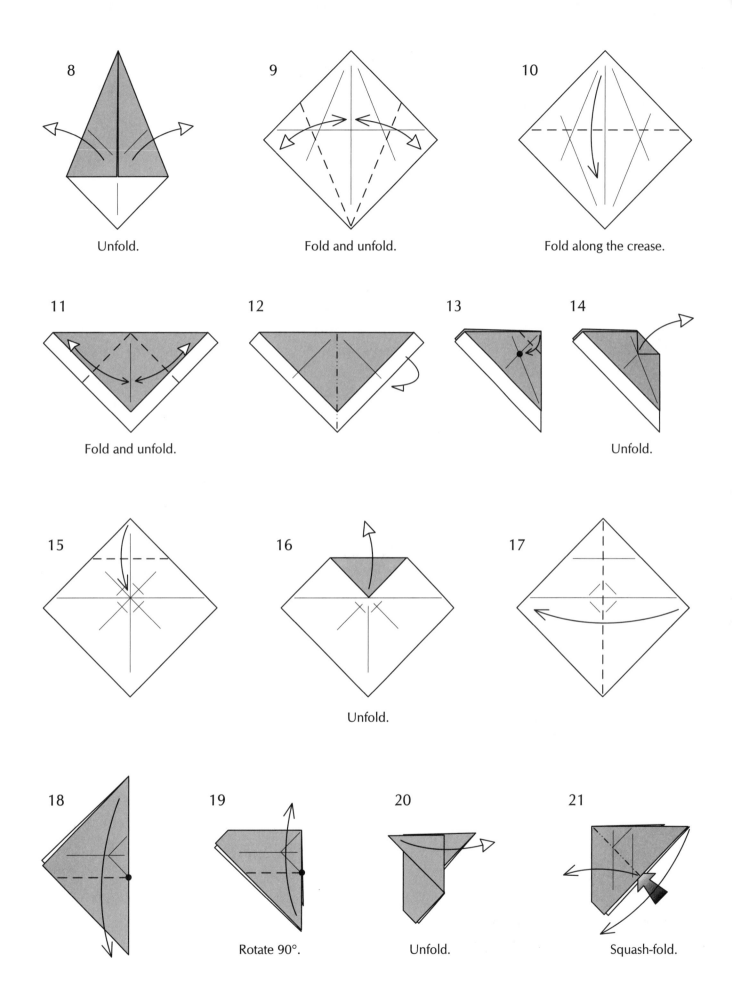

8

Unfold.

9

Fold and unfold.

10

Fold along the crease.

11

Fold and unfold.

12

13

14

Unfold.

15

16

Unfold.

17

18

19

Rotate 90°.

20

Unfold.

21

Squash-fold.

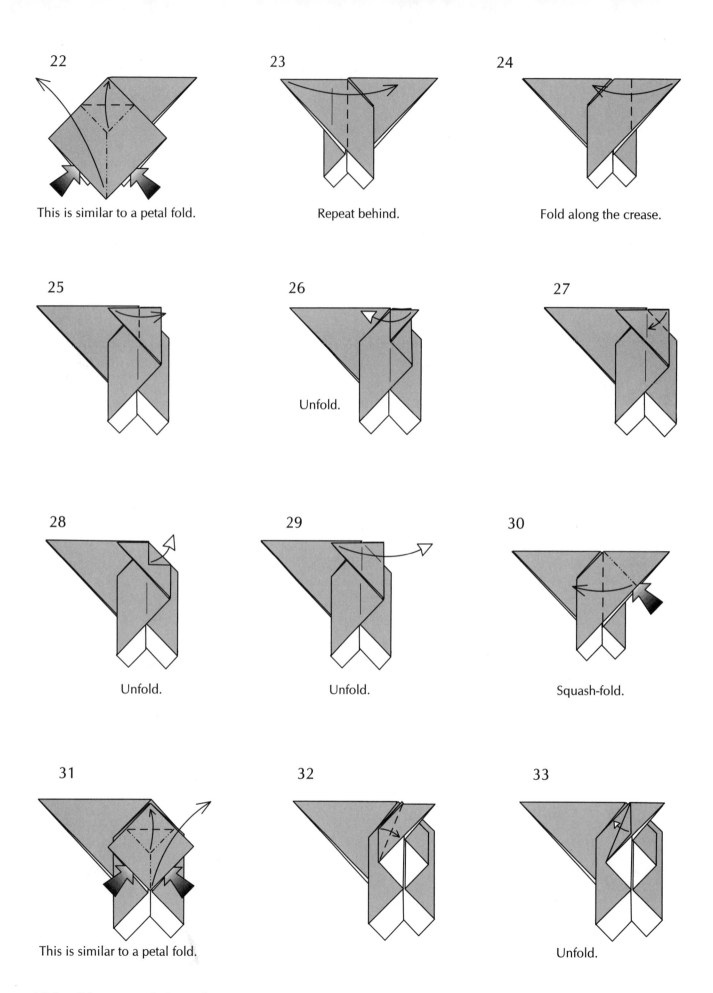

22

This is similar to a petal fold.

23

Repeat behind.

24

Fold along the crease.

25

26

Unfold.

27

28

Unfold.

29

Unfold.

30

Squash-fold.

31

This is similar to a petal fold.

32

33

Unfold.

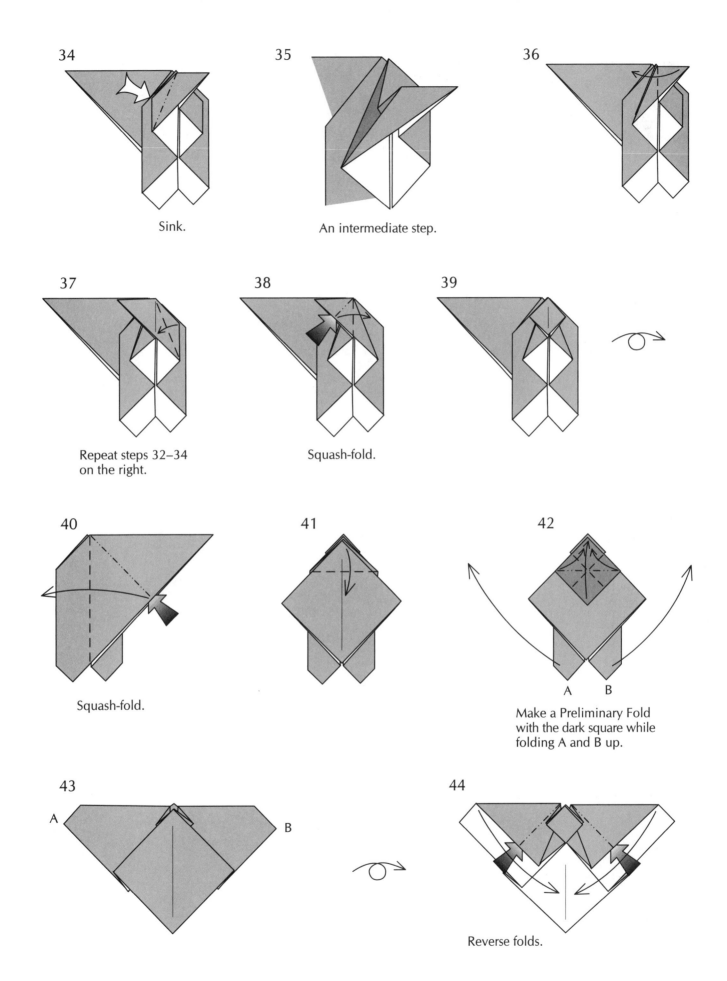

34

Sink.

35

An intermediate step.

36

37

Repeat steps 32–34
on the right.

38

Squash-fold.

39

40

Squash-fold.

41

42

A   B

Make a Preliminary Fold
with the dark square while
folding A and B up.

43

A                    B

44

Reverse folds.

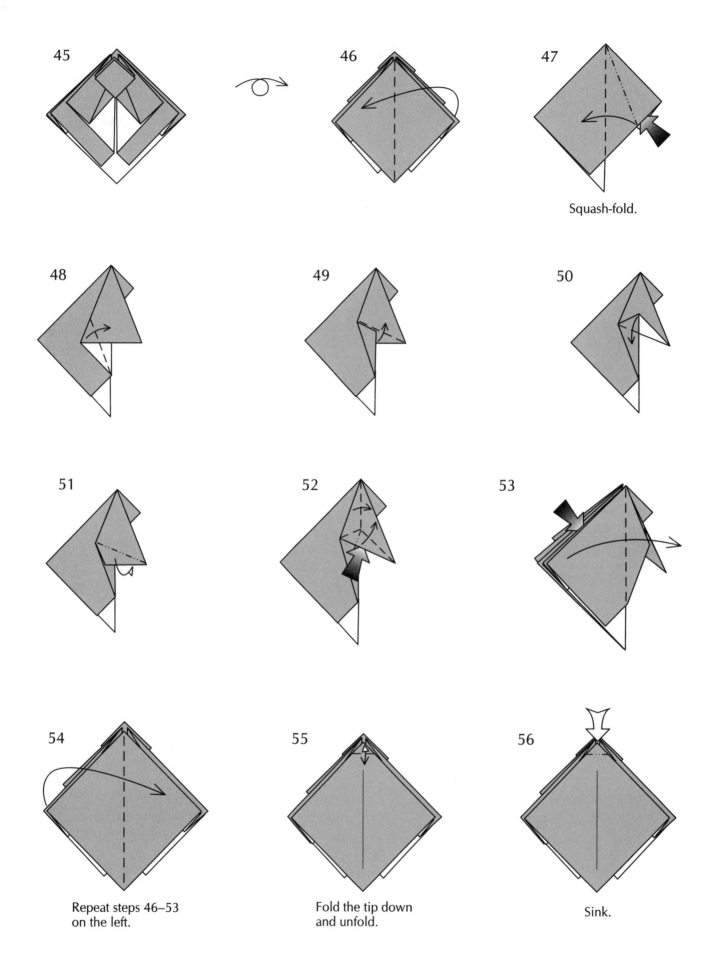

45

46

47

Squash-fold.

48

49

50

51

52

53

54

Repeat steps 46–53
on the left.

55

Fold the tip down
and unfold.

56

Sink.

57

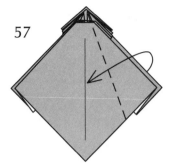

58

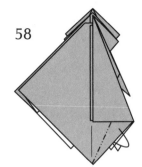

59

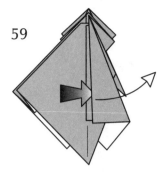

Unfold the top layer.

60

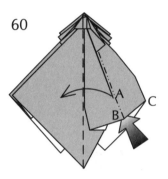

This is 3D. Puff out at A.

61

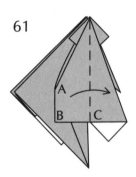

62

Repeat steps 57–61 on the left.

63

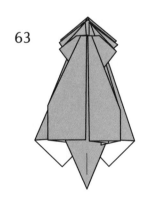

64

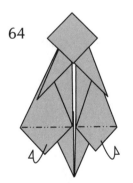

65

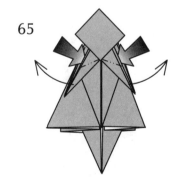

Reverse folds.

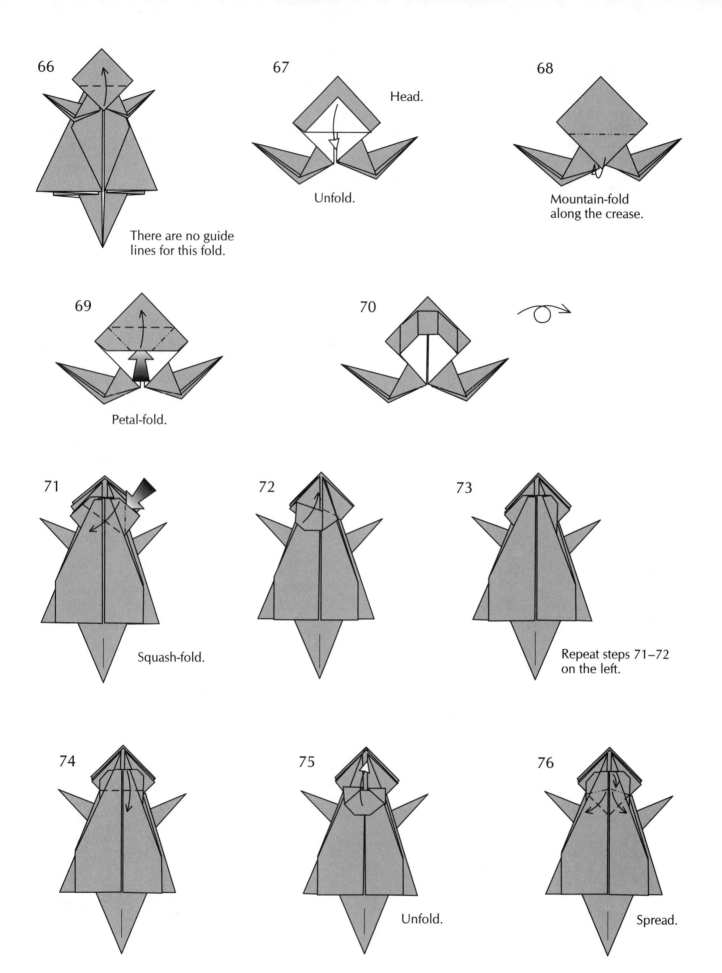

66 There are no guide lines for this fold.

67 Head. Unfold.

68 Mountain-fold along the crease.

69 Petal-fold.

70

71 Squash-fold.

72

73 Repeat steps 71–72 on the left.

74

75 Unfold.

76 Spread.

**77**

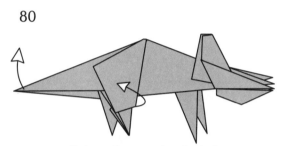

Reverse folds.

**78**

Lift the crown up
while folding in half.

**79**

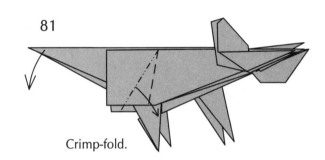

Crimp-fold.

**80**

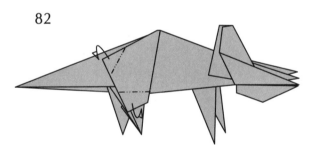

Pull the tail out and unlock the paper
by the hind legs. Repeat behind.

**81**

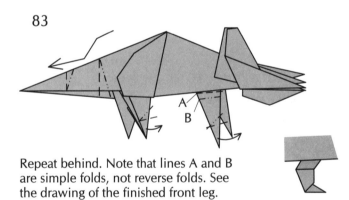

Crimp-fold.

**82**

Repeat behind.

**83**

A
B

Repeat behind. Note that lines A and B
are simple folds, not reverse folds. See
the drawing of the finished front leg.

**84**

Head.

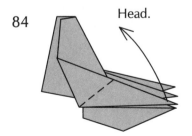

Repeat behind.

**85**

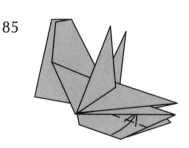

Repeat behind.

**86**

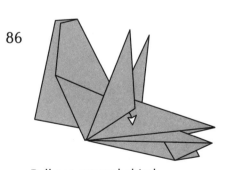

Pull out, repeat behind.

87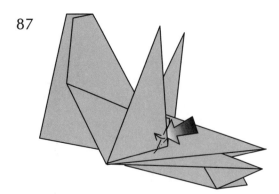

Squash-fold to form the
eye, repeat behind.

88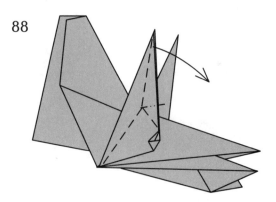

Rabbit-ear, repeat behind.

89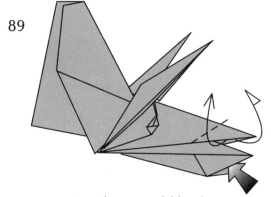

Outside-reverse-fold to form
a horn. Open the mouth.

90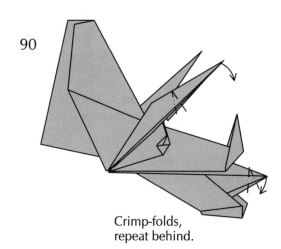

Crimp-folds,
repeat behind.

91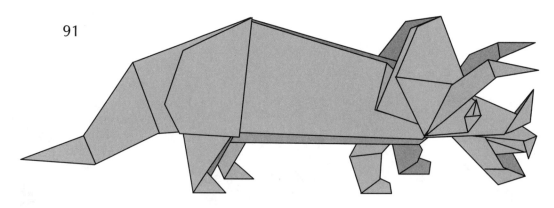

Triceratops

# Stegosaurus

steg-oh-SAW-rus

This unique dinosaur was 29 feet long and lived in the Jurassic and early Cretaceous. The plates on its back were to regulate its body heat. It had two walnut size brains. One brain was in its head and the other was at the base of its tail. This "roof lizard" was found in the western U.S. and ate plants.

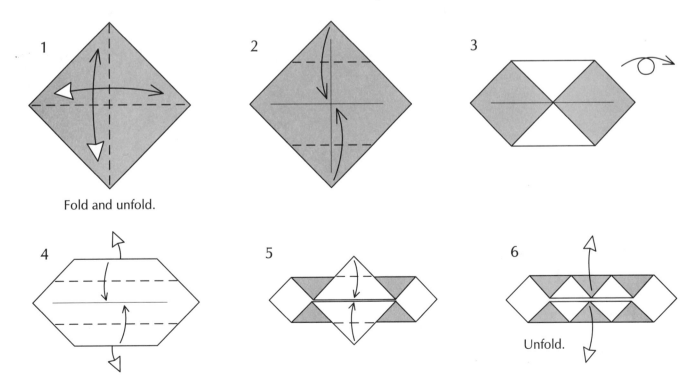

1 Fold and unfold.

2

3

4

5

6 Unfold.

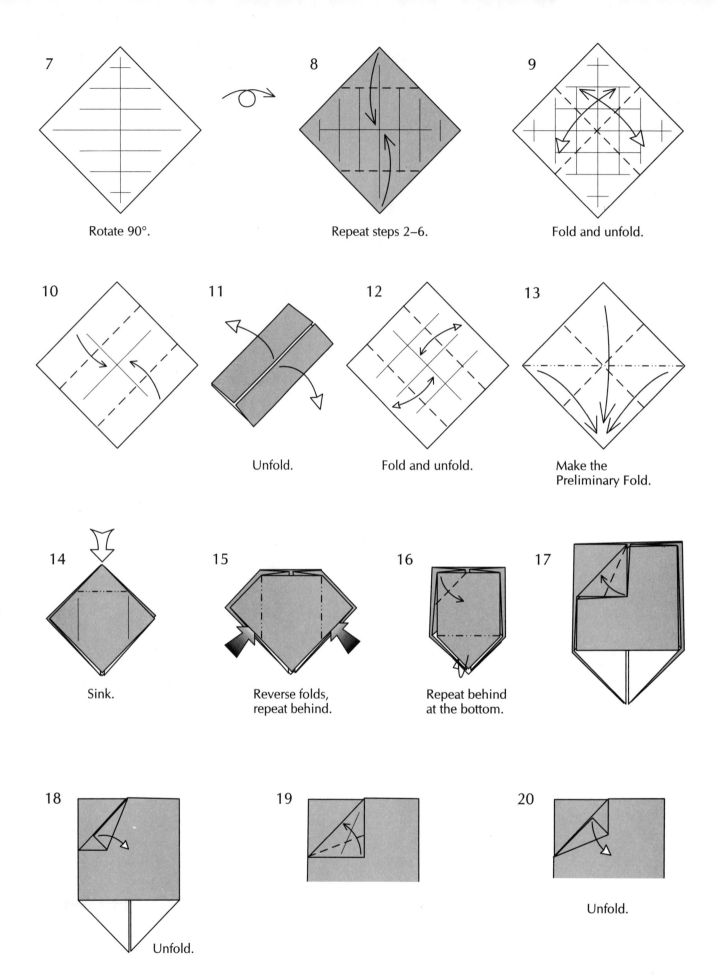

**7**

Rotate 90°.

**8**

Repeat steps 2–6.

**9**

Fold and unfold.

**10**

**11**

Unfold.

**12**

Fold and unfold.

**13**

Make the
Preliminary Fold.

**14**

Sink.

**15**

Reverse folds,
repeat behind.

**16**

Repeat behind
at the bottom.

**17**

**18**

Unfold.

**19**

**20**

Unfold.

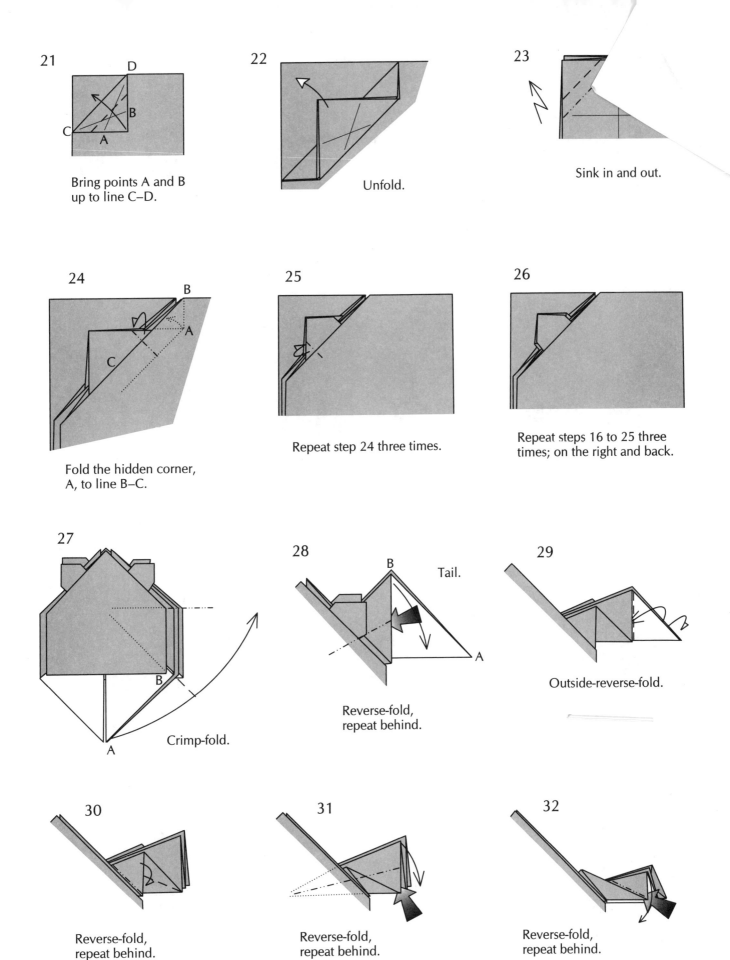

**21**

Bring points A and B up to line C–D.

**22**

Unfold.

**23**

Sink in and out.

**24**

Fold the hidden corner, A, to line B–C.

**25**

Repeat step 24 three times.

**26**

Repeat steps 16 to 25 three times; on the right and back.

**27**

Crimp-fold.

**28**

Tail.

Reverse-fold, repeat behind.

**29**

Outside-reverse-fold.

**30**

Reverse-fold, repeat behind.

**31**

Reverse-fold, repeat behind.

**32**

Reverse-fold, repeat behind.

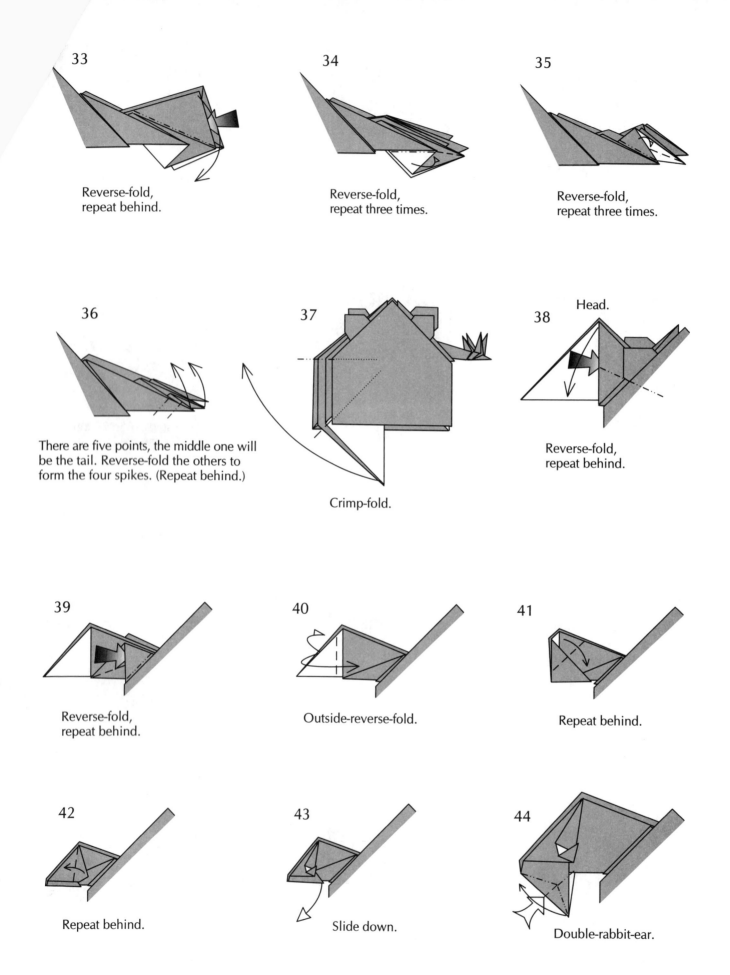

**33**

Reverse-fold,
repeat behind.

**34**

Reverse-fold,
repeat three times.

**35**

Reverse-fold,
repeat three times.

**36**

There are five points, the middle one will
be the tail. Reverse-fold the others to
form the four spikes. (Repeat behind.)

**37**

Crimp-fold.

**38**

Head.

Reverse-fold,
repeat behind.

**39**

Reverse-fold,
repeat behind.

**40**

Outside-reverse-fold.

**41**

Repeat behind.

**42**

Repeat behind.

**43**

Slide down.

**44**

Double-rabbit-ear.

# Gryposaurus

GRIP-oh-SAWR-us

This 30 foot long dinosaur lived near rivers where it ate water plants. Its name means "hook-nosed lizard". When this member of the hadrosaur family's teeth in its duck bill ground down and fell out, new teeth took their place. Fossils have been found in Alberta, Canada. It lived in the Cretaceous Period.

Begin with step 16 of Sphaerotholus (page 73).

1

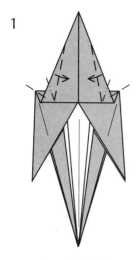

Squash folds.

2

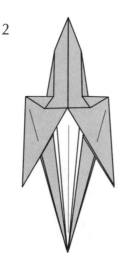

3

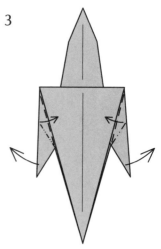

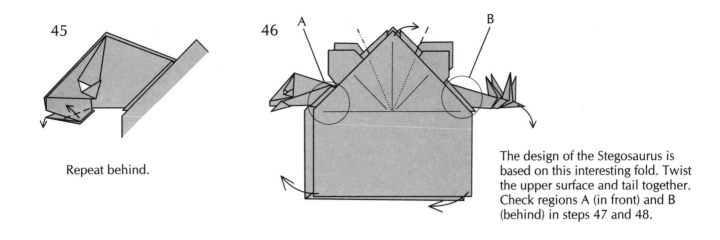

45

Repeat behind.

46

The design of the Stegosaurus is based on this interesting fold. Twist the upper surface and tail together. Check regions A (in front) and B (behind) in steps 47 and 48.

*Since the folding is no longer symmetrical, be sure to orient your model according to the drawings.*

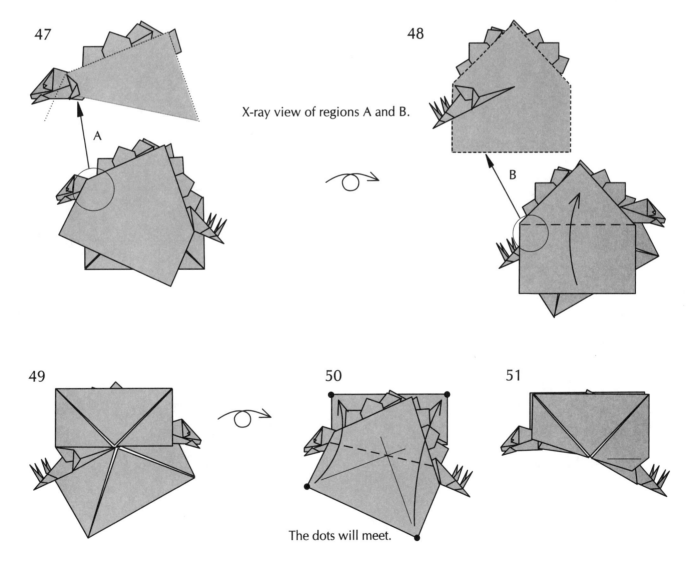

47

48

X-ray view of regions A and B.

49

50

The dots will meet.

51

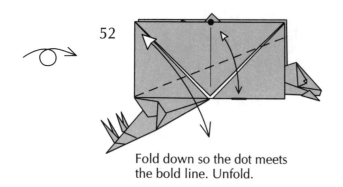

52

Fold down so the dot meets
the bold line. Unfold.

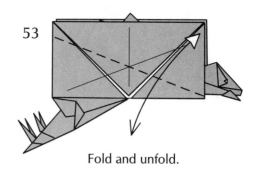

53

Fold and unfold.

54

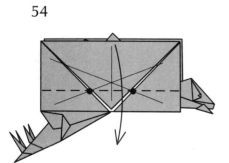

55

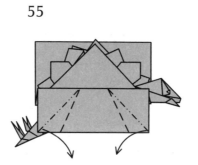

56

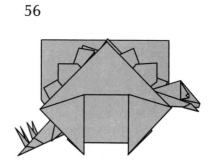

57

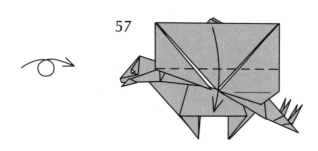

58

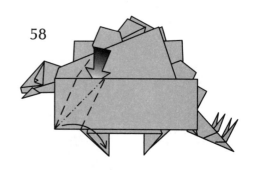

59

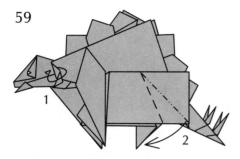

1. Fold inside-out to form
   a plate near the head.
2. Form a leg.

60

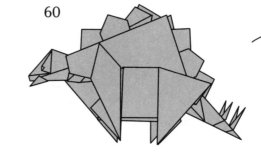

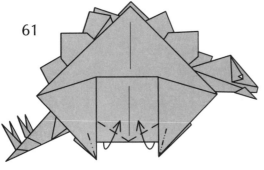

61

Repeat behind.

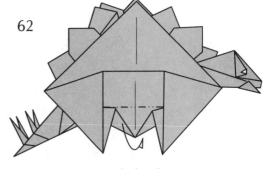

62

Repeat behind.

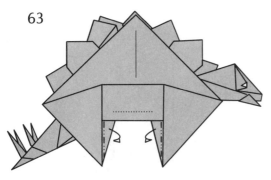

63

Mountain-fold on the x-ray
line, repeat behind.

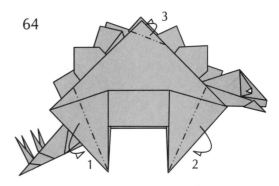

64

Fold behind at 1, 2, and 3.

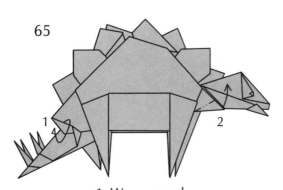

65

1. Wrap around.
2. Form a plate.

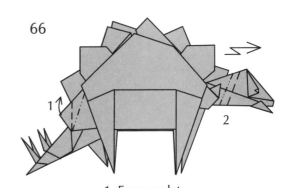

66

1. Form a plate.
2. Crimp-fold.

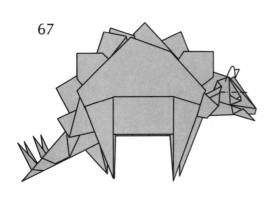

67

Repeat behind.

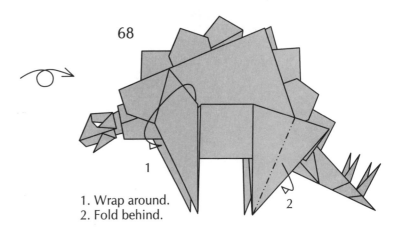

68

1. Wrap around.
2. Fold behind.

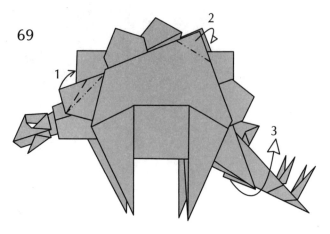

69

1. Form a plate.
2. Fold behind.
3. Pull out.

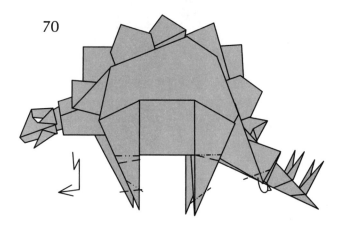

70

Repeat behind.

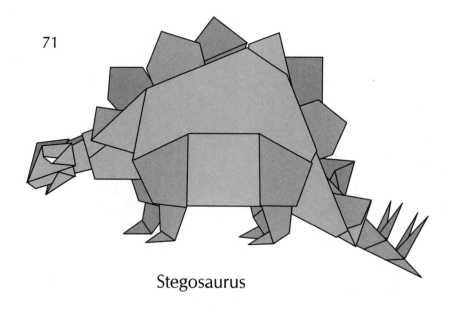

71

Stegosaurus